From Kid to Superkid

From Kid to Superkid

SET YOUR FAMILY ON THE PATH TO A JUNK-FOOD FREE, HEALTHY FUTURE

Paul Sacher

With recipes by Kate McBain

1 3 5 7 9 10 8 6 4 2

First published in the United Kingdom in 2005 by Vermilion,
an imprint of Ebury Publishing
Random House UK Ltd.
Random House
20 Vauxhall Bridge Road
London SW1V 2SA

Random House Australia (Pty) Limited
20 Alfred Street, Milsons Point, Sydney,
New South Wales 2061, Australia

Random House New Zealand Limited
18 Poland Road, Glenfield,
Auckland 10, New Zealand

Random House (Pty) Limited
Endulini, 5A Jubilee Road, Parktown 2193, South Africa

Random House UK Limited Reg. No. 954009
www.randomhouse.co.uk
Papers used by Vermilion are natural, recyclable products
made from wood grown in sustainable forests.

A CIP catalogue record is available for this
book from the British Library.

ISBN: 0091902525

Designed and typeset by seagulls

Printed and bound in Great Britain by
Mackays of Chatham plc, Chatham, Kent

The information given in this book is given in good faith and belief in its accuracy at the time of publication and may be subject to change. In addition, the advice offered in this book is not intended to be a substitute for the advice and counsel of your personal physician. Always consult a medical practitioner before embarking on a diet, or a course of exercise. Neither the author nor the publisher can be held responsible for any loss or claim arising out of the use, or misuse, of the information and suggestions contained in this book, or the failure to take medical advice.

To my parents Clive and Annette

Contents

Acknowledgements

To my loving grandparents who never imagined they would have an author for a grandson. David, for your never-ending enthusiasm, optimism and support. Mandy Sacher, who assisted me in writing this book and compiling the case studies, and who tackled every task head on while supporting me from initiation to completion of this book. Chris Calitz, my trusted friend, agent and confidant. Harry MacMillan and Ulla Stauch for believing in me and joining me in making the MEND Programme come to life. Dr Paul Chadwick for providing me with insight and information on changing behaviours. Clare Gray for compiling the GI tables. Anthony Hawser for planting the seed all those years ago. Kate McBain for creating all the delicious, low-GI recipes. Dominique, my friends, family and colleagues at the Institute of Child Health for testing all the recipes. Dr Margaret Lawson for supporting me in my research at the Institute of Child Health and proofing this book. Professor Tim Cole for advising me on the BMI and overall health risk tables. Julia Kellaway, my editor, Fiona MacIntyre, Amanda Hemmings and the rest of the Vermilion team for bringing my work to life. My colleagues at Great Ormond Street Hospital for Children for their advice and support, and all the familiesI have worked with over the last nine years for providing the material for the case studies.

Preface

Speaking from experience

Before I start, I think it's important that I share my own childhood with you. This will give you an insight into my life as an obese child and show how it has affected me.

As a young kid I was very skinny. I was a typical active child and fortunate to have the opportunity to spend a lot of time outdoors riding my bike and swimming. I was never naturally good at competitive physical sports, such as football, rugby and cricket, but preferred more mentally stimulating pursuits, such as chess, creating potions with my chemistry set, collecting Matchbox cars, entertaining my family with my wide array of magic tricks, and saving imaginary worlds with my Star Wars figurines. I also loved nature and wildlife and spent many hours nurturing anything from silk worms to sea monkeys and hamsters.

Then, at around the age of 11, puberty arrived and my hormones kicked in. This was a very confusing time and I remember watching my body change almost before my eyes. I started to shoot up in height and at the same time developed a voracious appetite – as most children do when they are going through a period of rapid growth. As is common with a lot of children, I loved sweets, chocolates, crisps and spending hours in front of the television or playing computer games. I wasn't given many unhealthy 'treats' at home – they were only handed out at weekends and as rewards – so I would simply buy them for myself on the way home from school and consume them in the privacy of my bedroom. I started to gain excessive weight and became very self-conscious of my body. I used to dread PE at school and the thought of changing in front of my peers and exposing my rolls of fat, suffering the humiliation of being the last person to be picked for the team, and being so out of breath during cross-country runs that I thought I was going to faint. In my mind, my PE teachers filled the spectrum from trolls and ogres, to evil witches and warlocks. PE was torture for me and I did anything I could do to avoid it. Strange how my mysterious illnesses always developed the night before PE! Lack of exercise combined with my extremely unhealthy appetite and love of high-sugar and high-fat foods saw my weight soar until I reached obesity level.

At this point I developed health problems that were directly linked to my excessive weight. I had asthma, and joint problems in my legs and feet, which made exercise even more difficult, and so the cycle continued. I became increasingly hostile towards my parents as a result of normal teenage rebellion combined with additional feelings of anger as a result of my weight and poor self-esteem. In her desperation, my mother took me to see a dietitian who put me on a calorie-restricted diet. At the time, that was what the medical profession believed was the correct treatment for obesity. I was told exactly what I should and shouldn't eat and was weighed on a weekly basis. I became obsessed with my weight and weighed myself every morning and sometimes in the evening as well. I felt victimised at family meals, where I was prepared separate low-calorie meals, while the rest of my family ate their normal meals.

My younger brother had always excelled at tennis and so he needed a fairly high-calorie diet, owing to the demands of his sport, and was allowed to eat whatever he liked. After a match he was often treated to ice cream sundaes and waffles. I, on the other hand, was extremely inactive and so required much less in the way of food and drinks and so was denied the same gastronomic pleasures. At this young age, I was not able to fully understand the reasons for the difference. I interpreted the way my parents treated me as a sign that I was less loved, less good and the failure of the family. I became increasingly isolated from the rest of my family. I dreaded the weekly weigh-ins at the dietitian. Needless to say, I did not lose weight – I gained it. Being told every week that my weight had increased only made me feel more like a failure, and further eroded my fragile self-esteem. After about three months of seeing the dietitian, my mother realised what a negative effect this was having on my confidence and the visits stopped. At this point she probably thought that it was better for me to be happy and fat than unhappy trying to be thin. Looking back on this period, it did raise my awareness of the difference between healthy and unhealthy foods but did not address how to change my eating behaviours. Dieting, for me, made the whole situation much worse and only helped to worsen my self-image and self-confidence.

My weight problem deteriorated as I got older and my obese teenage years are full of memories of feeling fat and ugly and always being ashamed of my body. On my summer holidays at the beach I was the big kid swimming in a T-shirt, thinking that it would hide my large body. In fact, it probably just drew more attention to the fact that I was hiding something! I remember shopping with my mother and really struggling to find clothes that would fit. A comment made when I tried on a striped shirt – 'people who are a bit overweight shouldn't wear horizontal stripes' – left me mortally wounded. Although I knew I was large, was I really that fat? This was the question that continually filled my head.

I was chronically depressed during these years. Not much inspired me, and life at home was hard as I took out all my anger and frustrations on my family. The more they told me what to eat and what not to eat the more I thought they were picking on me and didn't love me. The weight continued to pile on. One area that particularly worried me was my chest, as my breasts were prominent and this seriously affected my self-esteem.

Despite this, I still managed to achieve decent grades. University for me – at the age of 17 in a different city from my family – signified independence and a fresh start. I developed a voracious appetite of a different kind – not for food, but for knowledge to treat my condition. I absorbed as much information on diet and health as I could. This, combined with my science, nutrition and dietetic degrees, gave me the tools I needed to overcome my weight problem. I formulated my own ideas and combined everything I learnt into a simple yet effective plan for losing and maintaining my weight. I joined the local gym, started attending yoga classes with a friend, and even took up swimming again – a sport I had enjoyed in the past. As I became better at yoga, the instructor began to use me to demonstrate yoga positions to new attendees. This really helped to boost my self-confidence and encouraged me to try other activities in the gym. For the first time, exercise became an integral and even enjoyable part of my life. This regular activity, plus a few small changes in the way I was eating, led to my excessive weight falling off.

Although I had learnt for myself how to improve unhealthy eating and poor physical activity patterns, I realised that it took a lot of hard work and effort. I wondered how I could help children learn these same skills – but at a much younger age. I knew from my medical training that dieting is dangerous for children and realised that it was more important to get children into good, healthy habits early on in life. I never wanted another child to go through the difficulties I experienced in my childhood and so I began learning about the psychology of children and the most effective techniques to change their behaviours without risking setting them up for failure and reducing their self-esteem and confidence. I learnt about cognitive behavioural therapy and behavioural modification techniques, which help children to improve their behaviours in fun and achievable ways.

While this was a very lonely, difficult struggle, I do not regret it. Without this life-experience, I would not be in the position to share my experiences and my knowledge with you and your family. The advice in this book is based on my life experience as an obese child, combined with my medical and nutritional knowledge, my work as a specialist dietitian at Great Ormond Street Hospital for Children and my scientific knowledge researching childhood obesity treatments.

I hope that you will find this book life-changing and that it will give you an insight into the minds of your children who may be experiencing some of the things I felt as a child.

Prologue

Raising kids is not easy and doing the right thing by your children is important to all parents. The way parents raise their children is a product of their own upbringing, education, values and perceptions of right and wrong. The first thing to realise is that no parent is perfect, we all make mistakes. I have not written this book to teach you to be a parent, as I am not an expert in being a parent. What I can do is help you to understand what it is like to be an overweight child by using my own personal experiences as an overweight child, case studies of real-life situations, my knowledge on nutrition, as well as my research into the treatment of childhood obesity and how to combat it, in order to give you the tools to really make a difference in your children's lives.

This book is designed to give you a glimpse into the life of overweight kids and how this problem can affect them, not only in childhood but right into adulthood. Apart from all the health risks with which the media constantly bombard us, being overweight has other important impacts, such as low self-esteem and low levels of confidence, which are just as serious and also need to be dealt with effectively.

Raising healthy kids is a real challenge in today's world. Through my own life-experience, combined with my education as a dietitian and childhood obesity researcher, I have designed practical and effective tools that can help you to instigate a healthy life for you and your family – and to maintain it. My advice is simple and easy to follow and it will help you to wade through all the information out there and decide for yourself what is healthy and what is not. You don't have to be an expert in nutrition to learn how to read a food label and decipher whether a food belongs on your child's plate or is best left on the supermarket shelf. I have included a section to help you understand how active you and your children should be and I will show you easy ways to get them off the sofa and help to change their couch-potato lifestyles for good. Another important area of focus is the section dealing with behaviour modification techniques and self-esteem. This section contains many examples of how to motivate and encourage your children to eat that extra bit of fruit or walk the dog without having a world war breaking out at home.

Introduction

Facing the facts

If you follow the advice in this book you will be giving your children the best possible start in life. We know that children who are well nourished have improved levels of concentration and so perform better at school. We also know that children who are overweight have lower levels of self-esteem and confidence and higher levels of depression than healthy-weight children. So this book is aimed at all parents out there with children over the age of five years who want to transform their kid into a superkid.

Aim

The aim of this book is to improve your family's health using the latest advances in nutrition, exercise and behavioural modification, integrating them into a simple, yet effective, lifestyle programme that will serve as a foundation for healthy living for their entire lives. This book will help you to prevent your children becoming a part of the obesity statistics and will also help those

Did you know?

It is predicted that by the year 2020, one in three adults and one in five children in the UK will be obese!

who already have overweight or obese children. This book will help you to understand what it's like for overweight children, what goes on in their minds and how what you may think is the best way to help your children could be doing more harm than good.

How to use this book

This book contains a wealth of information aimed at improving your children's diet and making sure that the foods they eat set them up for good health for their entire life. It is not about putting your children on a special diet. Rather it is about improving the foods that your entire family eats. It contains great ideas and tips to get your kids off the couch and inspire them to be *more* physically active and to *enjoy* being active. You will also learn to identify if your children are depressed and how to improve their self-esteem and confidence.

Unlike other diet and lifestyle books, this book will explain not only how to follow the healthiest of eating plans but also how to get your children to change their unhealthy habits and behaviour. I will explain the SMART way of encouraging healthy habits and behaviour using simple techniques such as goals and rewards and how to avoid factors in your children's everyday lives that trigger unhealthy behaviour.

Learn about low-GI eating, reducing unhealthy fats, sugar and salt in your children's diet, ways to get them more active and the tools to transform them from kids into superkids.

Background

Obesity is all around us – in newspapers and magazines, on the radio, television, the Internet – and on the high street. Why the fuss? Surely a bit of fat – apart from maybe not looking very attractive on the beach – won't do us any harm? Wrong. Excessive fat is damaging to health and obesity is on the increase. In fact, obesity is fast becoming the number one killer. Sadly obesity not only affects adults but has begun to affect increasing numbers of children too. Worldwide we are seeing many more young people becoming overweight and even obese, more so than ever before in history. However, besides the health risks, being an overweight kid is not easy – trust me, I have been there.

Being overweight as a child caused me health problems and led to problems at school, feelings of inadequacy and isolation, and damaged my relationships with my parents and teachers. Unfortunately, Western society treats overweight people differently. We are conditioned from birth that fat is bad. In one study, published in 1995, children as young as four years old said they regarded overweight children as being mean, ugly, less intelligent, lazy, selfish, dishonest and a poor choice of friends. In the same study, healthy-weight children were rated as clever, attractive, healthy, kind, happy and popular.

Obesity is a high-profile subject. It is frequently on the television news and in the newspapers. It is the topic of reality shows and political discussions and is the subject of much scientific research. In fact, obesity is all around us at the moment; one just has to look around when walking down the street. Never has the human race faced such a potentially serious health problem. The issue is not about fatness itself, but the consequences of lugging this extra weight around and the effects it has on our poor bodies that have to adapt to the heavy load. This additional baggage comes at a serious cost to our health.

All parents want what's best for their kids and watching their children following an unhealthy diet and being physically inactive can be heart-breaking. Many parents struggle to teach their youngsters to be healthy because children only worry about the here and now – the newest, coolest video game; the next set of exams; the upcoming holiday – not the state of their health in the distant future. Being unhealthy does not necessarily affect children straight away but often causes problems later on in life. Therefore, it is important for parents to lead the way and make sure their children are leading healthy lifestyles from the start – rather than trying to change them later on. This can be very difficult – especially as many parents do not follow a healthy lifestyle themselves. It is far harder to tell a child to do something if you don't do it yourself. 'Do as I say and not as I do' is an approach that few children respond to positively. Children learn by example, and so how you choose to live your life as a parent is one of the most important factors in determining how they will live theirs.

This may all sound like a 'no win' situation but there are many ways to improve health and overcome obesity, which I will guide you towards in this book. No advice in this book is beyond the reach of anybody. It is simple and practical. The advice is intended for the whole family – the only way to raise a superkid is to be a superfamily. Try to read the entire book, even if you think you know a lot about a particular subject discussed. You will be surprised how many common misperceptions there are about nutrition and exercise. Because eating is a daily occurrence, many people think they are experts on nutrition. However, with an abundance of fad diets and confusing nutritional information in most of the mainstream magazines and on the television, a lot of people have some very strange ideas about what is healthy and what is not. You do not have to be a vegetarian, organic-eating, soya-milk drinking, wheat-grass growing, supplement-popping junkie to be healthy – in fact, quite the opposite. Good nutrition is not only simple and easy, it is also cheaper than eating unhealthily – something that will come as a surprise to many people.

Children learn so much at school today, but where do they go to learn the basic skills needed to follow a healthy lifestyle? The answer is not a simple one. It is not one person's, or one establishment's, responsibility to teach children to be healthy. It is the responsibility of society as a whole to make sure that being healthy is the easiest option for all of us. Healthy lifestyle education starts at home and continues throughout our lives in the wider world.

The advice in this book will help you to raise your children in the healthiest possible way. No matter what state their health is in at present, there is always room for improvement.

Is your problem unique?

The answer is a definite no! Worldwide there are now approximately 155 million overweight or obese school-age children. According to the World Health Organization, childhood obesity has reached epidemic proportions. The most recent Health Survey for England (2002) showed that in children aged 2–15, 16 per cent were obese and almost a third (30 per cent) were either overweight or obese. Applied throughout the UK, it means that around 2.4 million children are affected by overweight, including 700,000 who are obese. In the UK, almost half of men (47 per cent) and one-third of women (33 per cent) are overweight. Approximately one-fifth (21 per cent) of men and one-quarter (24 per cent) of women are obese.

The current childhood obesity problem is worst in the Americas, followed by Europe, Near/Middle East, Asia-Pacific and then, last but not least, sub-Saharan Africa. Another important factor is the rapid rate at which the number of obese kids has increased. Over the last decade the problem of childhood obesity

Did you know?

In a study in the British Medical Journal 40 per cent of overweight mothers and 45 per cent of overweight fathers rated their own weight as being 'about right,' while 27 per cent of overweight mothers and 61 per cent of overweight fathers were unconcerned about their weight.

has doubled, and if this trend continues for the next decade we are going to see huge numbers of obese children. That is why the time is right to do something about the problem now.

If this is not a diet book, what is it?

If you are looking for a healthy rapid-weight-loss diet, or some other type of healthy quick-fix solution for your children or yourself, the bad news is that it does not exist – not in this book, nor anywhere else for that matter. In order to correct bad habits and improve health you have to change your behaviour – the types of food you eat and the amount of physical activity you do. This is a lifestyle approach, aimed at correcting years of unhealthy behaviour and keeping you and your children healthy for the rest of your lives.

Weight-loss diets do not work in the long term, and can do a lot more harm than good. It is not hard to lose weight in the short term; we have all done it many times. The hard part is keeping the weight off. With children, losing weight rapidly is not recommended for health reasons. Children are not 'mini-adults', they are still growing and so restricting their intake of nutrients or food could have a serious effect on their health. For example, many teenage girls restrict dairy products in the belief that these foods are fattening. This can lead to low calcium intake at a time when bones are growing extremely fast, and can result in brittle bones later on in life when it is much too late to reverse the condition. Never forget – children need balanced

Did you know?

A study in 2003 found that the more children and teenagers dieted the more likely they were to become obese as adults.

diets, and so restricting their intake by putting them on a rapid weight loss diet is dangerous to their health.

So, if weight-loss diets don't work, what does? Well, we know that for children to grow healthily they need a good, balanced, varied diet that includes foods from all the different food groups. This will supply their growing bodies with all the building blocks needed for life. We also know that to *be* healthy and to *stay* healthy it is very important for children and adults to be physically active. So really, it's about learning how to eat healthier and to include physical activity in your daily routine. This book is filled with ideas to improve diet and to increase physical activity. These changes are required for life and so this is called 'a lifestyle programme'.

Worried you may not be able to follow all the advice in this book? If you were able to practise every recommendation in this book, you would most certainly be a superparent. All that I hope is that you make some small changes to your family's lifestyle in order to improve their health – while ensuring that nobody feels like they are on a diet, or that your home has changed into a 'boot camp' overnight. A section of this book deals with helping you to change your children's behaviour so that they are more likely to listen to your suggestions to improve their health.

Part One

What's the Problem?

Chapter 1

Are my children a healthy weight, overweight or obese?

Being able to tell if your children are a healthy weight or not is extremely hard. For most parents, if their children look well and happy, then they would usually assume everything is fine. Sometimes it takes a comment from a friend or relative to make one start to worry. For example, 'Lisa's growing very fast, hopefully she will grow into her puppy fat' or 'James is a really big boy, he must be a great rugby player?' Sometimes children will come home from school and say they have been teased or bullied because of their appearance and, more commonly, their weight. Children are incredibly insensitive and heavier children can often take a huge emotional (and sometimes even physical) beating from their peers.

When I use the words 'healthy weight', 'overweight' or 'obese', I am referring to the Body Mass Index (BMI) – see pages 22–27). BMI is a medical definition related to height and weight

What does obesity mean?

Obesity is a medical term and it means someone's weight has reached the point where it is likely to cause serious health problems in the future. Examples of health problems caused by being obese are: cancer, heart disease, diabetes and depression.

only. It is not based on how people appear, or what society deems to be a healthy weight. The BMI is created using measurements taken from many UK children and gives a good indication of whether a child is a healthy weight or not. There are always exceptions – if you are concerned, please speak to your GP. Many of the people that children adore and aspire to be like, such as pop idols and film stars, are often classified medically as 'underweight'. Sports stars too are not your 'average person'. So they should not be held up as examples for your children.

So how do you tell whether your children are a healthy weight or not? You probably have some idea but as children are growing it is hard to know for sure. Even for experts like myself, it is difficult simply to look at a child and know whether he or she is a healthy weight or not. Children generally are getting larger owing to an abundance of high-energy foods and a decrease in physical activity. Therefore the average weight of children is increasing and there are significantly more children at the upper end of the weight range and fewer at the lower end, as underweight is a much less common problem in medically healthy Western children. When I was an obese child, it was obvious that I had a weight problem as I was much larger than the majority of my peers. In fact, I knew for sure that I was the third fattest child at my school. Today, as many more children are large, it is more difficult to tell whether children are overweight by comparing them to their friends. Also, many parents shrug off the problem as they think that there are so many other children who are as overweight – if not more so – than their own children.

Another serious issue that the medical world is aware of is that many parents don't want to acknowledge that their children have a weight problem. Often this may mean parents acknowledging that they have a weight problem themselves. It can even be perceived by some parents as suggesting that they have failed at being a good parent. There is also some concern by parents that if they constantly focus on their children's weight they may cause them to develop an eating disorder later on, but there is little research to back this up. There is, however, research that suggests childhood obesity is associated with the development of eating disorders and that this risk is not increased by trying to help children overcome the problem. In fact, the significant medical risks associated with being obese are more serious than the small risk of causing an eating disorder in children by

Did you know?

In a study into parents' awareness of overweight in their children published in the British Medical Journal, only a quarter of those questioned recognised overweight in their children. Even when the child was obese, 33 per cent of mothers and 57 per cent of fathers saw their child's weight as 'about right'.

treating their weight problem. It is always important to remain supportive of your children and approach their weight problems with positive reinforcement and encouragement. I always recommend that *parents avoid criticism and negative talk* about their children's physical appearance and focus on the health benefits instead (see page 214).

Let me show you how to calculate whether or not you or your children are overweight. As children are still growing, you should check their weight and height at least every six months. That way you keep on top of any growth problems before they become serious.

What is the difference between 'overweight' and 'obese'?

Being 'overweight' as defined by the BMI table, means you are at risk of developing health problems due to your weight. It signifies caution for the future and should be seen as a warning sign to think about the food you are eating and the amount of activity you are doing and start making some changes. Being defined as 'obese' on the BMI table means that your weight is now at a point where it is *likely* to cause you health problems. It should be a very loud signal that it is time to start taking action in improving your diet and being more active.

The Body Mass Index (BMI)

The simplest and most practical way to establish whether your children are underweight, a healthy weight, overweight or obese

Did you know?

In some cultures, obesity is regarded as a sign of wealth and success. Unfortunately, even though it is socially acceptable to be obese, these people will still suffer poor health if their weight remains unchecked.

is to weigh them and measure their height. Once you have these figures you can use the body mass index (BMI) calculation shown overleaf. The calculation is the same for children and adults. However, it is very important that you use the children's table for children and the adults' table for adults. Bear in mind that some children and teenagers going through a 'growth spurt' will often fill out before they shoot up.

This method is fairly reliable, but there are exceptions. As BMI only takes into account your total body weight and not what that weight is comprised of, in some people, for example those with a lot of muscle rather than fat, their BMI could put them in the 'obese' range incorrectly. There are more sophisticated methods of measuring body composition, often used in gyms, health clubs and by dietitians and other health-care professionals trained in measuring body composition. Even more sophisticated methods exist for use mainly in research – these include full body scans that produce images of slices through the body. From these, you can calculate total amounts of fat, muscle, bone and other tissue.

Another really useful, practical measure of 'fatness' is your waist circumference (see page 28). Storing fat around your stomach is associated with hormonal problems and a higher risk of heart disease, so measuring your waist circumference will let you know whether you are in the high-health-risk category or not.

Once you have calculated your children's BMIs and waist circumference and your own, plot them on the table on page 30 to see your overall health risk. The BMI calculation for adults and children is:

$$\frac{\text{weight (kilograms)}}{\text{height x height (metres)}}$$

This means that an adult/child with a height of 1.7 metres (170 centimetres) and a weight of 70kg, has a BMI of 70 ÷ (1.7 x 1.7) = 24

Let's go through that again, step by step:

1. Measure the height in metres and multiply that figure by itself (e.g. 1.7 x 1.7).
2. Measure the weight in kilograms.
3. Divide the weight by the figure obtained in step 1 (height x height) to give the BMI.

Another example, you might be 1.6 metres tall and weigh 65kg. The first calculation would then be: 1.6 x 1.6 = 2.6. BMI would then be 65 divided by 2.6 = 25.

Children's BMI table

Once you have calculated your children's BMIs, plot them on the table overleaf according to their sex and age. For example, in the calculation above, if a girl is 14.5 years old and has a BMI of 24 she falls between the overweight and obese category, and so would be classified as overweight.

If a boy was 10 years old and had a BMI of 24 he would be classified as obese.

Using the table

Calculate your children's BMIs using the method described and then plot them on the table overleaf. If their BMI is less than the overweight column for their age they are a healthy weight. The closer their BMI is to the overweight value the more likely they are to be overweight. If the value is above the value in the over-weight column but below the value in the obese column then they are overweight. If the value falls on or above the number in the obese column then they are considered obese.

	OVERWEIGHT		OBESE	
Age (years)	Boys	Girls	Boys	Girls
5	17.4	17.1	19.3	19.2
5.5	17.5	17.2	19.5	19.3
6	17.6	17.3	19.8	19.7
6.5	17.7	17.5	20.2	20.1
7	17.9	17.8	20.6	20.5
7.5	18.2	18.0	21.1	21.0
8	18.4	18.3	21.6	21.6
8.5	18.8	18.7	22.2	22.2
9	19.1	19.1	22.8	22.8
9.5	19.5	19.5	23.4	23.5
10	19.8	19.9	24.0	24.1
10.5	20.2	20.3	24.6	24.8
11	20.6	20.7	25.1	25.4
11.5	20.9	21.2	25.6	26.1
12	21.2	21.7	26.0	26.7
12.5	21.6	22.1	26.4	27.2
13	21.9	22.6	26.8	27.8
13.5	22.3	23.0	27.2	28.2
14	22.6	23.3	27.6	28.6
14.5	23.0	23.7	28.0	28.9
15	23.3	23.9	28.3	29.1
15.5	23.6	24.2	28.6	29.3
16	23.9	24.4	28.9	29.4
16.5	24.2	24.5	29.1	29.6
17	24.5	24.7	29.4	29.7
17.5	24.7	24.8	29.7	29.8
18	25.0	25.0	30.0	30.0

Adapted from: Cole et al, 2000. *British Medical Journal.*

Adults' BMI table

For adults aged 18 years and above, use the table below to determine your own weight classification. Calculate the BMI as above and see where you fall.

Body Mass Index	Classification	Risk of disease associated with excess weight
Less than 18.5	Underweight	Low (but increased risk of other clinical problems)
19 to 24.9*	Desirable or healthy range	Average
25 to 29	Overweight	Increased
30–39	Obese	Moderate
40 or above	Extremely (morbidly) obese	Very severe

* See Did You Know? box below.
Source: World Health Organization.

Did you know?

The World Health Organization has concluded that the risk of obesity-related diseases among Asian men is greater in those with a BMI of 23 and above, and that this should be the benchmark for overweight in this population.

Waist measurements

This method uses your waist measurement to determine your fat distribution and hence your health risk. Use a non-stretch measuring tape. Make sure the child or adult is standing up straight. Find the narrowest point of the waist – usually about 2cm above the belly button. If this is difficult, ask the person to bend to the side and you will see a crease in the skin – this can be used as a the point for the measurement.

Using the table

Once you have measured their waist circumference, plot the value on the table opposite. If the value is less than the increased risk value then it represents a healthy waist measurement. But the closer the value gets to the 'increased-risk' value, so the health risk increases. If the value is above the 'increased-risk' value, but less than the 'high risk' value then the person is at an increased risk of poor health. If the value falls above the 'high-risk' value, then he or she is at a high risk of health problems.

Overall health risk

Once you have done the calculations above, use the table on page 30 to calculate the overall health risk that you and your family face. Follow the BMI result along and where it meets the waist circumference result, the figure in the box is your overall risk. For example, if your BMI result was 'overweight' and your waist circumference indicated 'increased risk' your overall health risk is 2.

Children's waist measurement (cm)

	INCREASED RISK		HIGH RISK	
Age	**Boys**	**Girls**	**Boys**	**Girls**
5	55.6	55.4	57.0	57.2
6	57.1	57.0	58.7	58.9
7	58.8	58.7	60.7	60.8
8	60.9	60.4	62.9	62.7
9	63.2	62.0	65.4	64.5
10	65.6	63.6	67.9	66.2
11	67.9	65.4	70.4	68.1
12	70.4	67.3	72.9	70.5
13	73.1	69.1	75.7	71.8
14	76.1	70.6	78.9	73.2
15	79.0	71.7	82.0	74.3
16	81.8	72.6	85.2	75.1

For 17 years and older use adult table values.

Adapted from: McCarthy, H.D., 2001. *European Journal of Clinical Nutrition.*

Adult's waist measurement (cm)

	INCREASED RISK	HIGH RISK
Men	94–101 Asian men: over 90	102 and above Asian men: over 102
Women	80–87	88 and above

	Waist circumference low risk	Waist circumference increased risk	Waist circumference high risk
BMI healthy weight	0	1	2
BMI overweight	1	2	3
BMI obese	2	3	4

A score of 0 means that you or your children are not currently at risk of health problems due to your weight or fat distribution. The advice in this book can therefore help to keep you healthy. A score above 0 means that your risk of health problems due to your weight or waist circumference is increased. As the value increases from 1 to 4, so does your risk of having serious health problems. Follow the advice in this book to prevent the serious health consequences that can result from being overweight and unhealthy. It is never too late to reverse poor eating and exercise habits.

My children are not overweight so why should I read any further?

Anyone can become overweight at any point in their life. For most people, it is much easier to gain weight than it is to lose weight. Once you have gained weight and then lost it, it is much easier to re-gain the weight – plus add more in the future. **Good nutrition is important for everyone, not only overweight people. Healthy eating and being physically active can reduce health risks and lengthen the life-span of the whole family.**

Chapter 2

What are the causes of the obesity epidemic?

There are many possible reasons for the current obesity epidemic in the West but the main ones relate to changes in the foods we are eating and in declining levels of physical activity. I think it is important to examine these reasons so that we can address the causes and, hopefully, prevent or minimise the problem for future generations.

Improved food technology, mass production and modernisation have brought about a situation where it is much easier to be unhealthy than it is to be healthy. Being healthy should be the easy option but it isn't. Unfortunately, it takes planning and concerted effort on a daily basis to make sure we don't fall into the trap of choosing the unhealthy option. Examples of this are all around us, such as a surplus of convenience food, designed to make life a lot easier and reduce the need to shop for fresh ingredients and cook for ourselves. 'Convenience food' sounds great but it is often packed full of excessive calories, heart-damaging types of fats, and loaded with sugar and salt.

Foods targeted at children, one might assume, would cater for children's nutritional needs – but quite the opposite is true. Many of these foods, too, are loaded with dangerous levels of fat, sugar and salt. It is important to try to teach children the skills necessary to shop and cook, thereby lessening their dependence on ready-made meals and junk foods. However, buying healthy foods is like tackling an obstacle course, avoiding aisle after aisle of refined, unhealthy foods. The foods worst for our children's health are often placed on the lower shelves to catch young eyes. Foods are attractively packaged with cartoon characters and bright colours – any trick to tempt the most innocent and persuadable.

Humans have done such a good job at adapting our environment to make life easier for ourselves that the amount of energy we take in as food easily exceeds the amount of energy we burn up through physical activity.

Our ancestors, the cavemen, had a very different life from ours. They used to hunt for meat and forage for fruit and vegetables. Hunting used lots of energy and kept them fit. In

Did you know?

- In 1950, the average supermarket had a choice of 5,000 food items.
- In 2000, the average supermarket had a choice of 30,000 food items.

addition, their diet was largely unprocessed and natural. Nowadays, we just have to pop out to the nearest convenience store or supermarket to find shelves packed full of seductive foods, many so adulterated by the manufacturing process that it is impossible to recognise their origins. If it was not for the ingredient lists, we probably wouldn't have a clue what we were eating. Products are stripped nutritionally, leaving refined, processed substitutes in place of wholesome food.

We are surrounded with food choices; there are fast-food outlets in abundance in all cities and towns. You do not even have to leave your home to sample the delights of foods from all around the world, delivery is the buzz-word and takeaway restaurants abound with exotic choices and menus. At the same time, our modern hectic lifestyle has led to snacking on the run and increased use of ready-made meals/convenience foods. This lifestyle change, combined with the decreasing nutritional value of modern foods, is slowly ruining our children's health and our own. We humans naturally have a taste for high-fat, sweet and salty foods. This is being preyed upon by the food manufacturers and the supermarkets which stock an abundance of such products – most being bad for our health.

Many modern-day pursuits for adults and children do not require much effort. Watching television requires so few calories that it can be thought of as a state similar to being asleep. When we are asleep our bodies use only enough energy to keep us alive without having to do much else. As the number of hours you sleep or watch television increases, so your activity levels and the amount of energy you burn up decrease.

Did you know?

Research has shown that foods prepared and cooked at home have fewer calories than foods in restaurants, fast-food outlets, at school and in the work canteen. The more meals you eat from such sources, the more likely you are to be overweight. Eat home-cooked foods whenever possible and try to eat as a family.

This makes it so much easier to gain weight without necessarily having to eat substantially more than you require. Other activities that contribute to this lack of activity are work and games using computers (sorry, but jostling joysticks or pushing buttons does not burn up much energy), DVD players, videos, lifts and escalators.

In many parts of our cities, it is much easier to jump in your car than battle on foot on routes designed with traffic and not humans in mind. In some places, you have to be both athlete and gymnast to overcome all the pedestrian barriers and cross wide traffic-filled streets. Our cities have not been designed to enable children to cycle to school in safety. It is far easier (and safer) to bundle them into the back of the car and drive them there.

It's no wonder we are the fattest we have ever been – and the problem is getting worse.

Manufacturers have worked tirelessly to produce low-cost, processed foods for consumers. But in processing foods, natural food ingredients are increasingly being replaced with modern-day fillers of lower nutritional quality. Healthy foods, such as corn, are processed into a final product, corn syrup, that is unrecognisable from its origins. Wholesome ingredients are left out in order to reduce manufacturing costs and boost profits. This manufacturing process may have some advantages, such as increasing the shelf life of products and improving 'mouth feel' and texture, but are these worth the large decrease in their nutritional value? Refining foods strips them of their goodness and

It's my genes that make me fat

People sometimes blame their genes for their weight problem. Overweight does tend to run in families, but is this genetics, or the fact that families tend to eat similar foods and do similar levels of activity? Well, genes do play a part. We know that some people are genetically tall and thin or short and stocky. But the rapid rise in obesity cannot be blamed on genes as it has happened so quickly. Genes tell your body where to store the fat – around your stomach or on the hips. Genes also make it easier for some people to put on weight. But with good eating and adequate levels of physical activity you can remain a healthy weight no matter what your genetic makeup. Changes due to genes take many generations before they become obvious, so the changes we are seeing now in obesity levels are definitely linked to other factors. It's not our genes that have changed, it's the foods that we are eating and the lack of physical activity in our lives that have brought about this problem.

leaves 'empty' calories – high in energy but with little of the vitamins, minerals, trace elements and fibre which are essential for good health and the proper functioning of our bodies.

So how do we get fat?

Many people are unhappy with their bodies. You will often hear people say that they are the type of person that 'easily puts weight on'. Well, the bad news is that our bodies are all pretty similar and if you take in more energy (food) than you burn up, your body has no choice but to store it as fat. We are all born with fat cells which can be thought of as balloons. Once you have the balloons you have them for life. Whenever the amount of food we take in is greater than the energy we burn up by being active, our bodies store this excess as fat in our 'ballooning' fat cells.

This is how people put on weight. If you continue to eat more than you burn up these fat cells eventually fill up and so your body has to produce more fat cells to store the excess. Our body also stores excess fat around our internal organs, and this is an additional health-risk factor. The waist circumference measurement (see page 29) health risk table is based on this fact. Those who store weight around their middle – the so-called 'apple shape' – are at greater risk of disorders such as heart disease than those who store fat around the hips and thighs – the so-called 'pear shape'.

When we lose fat, the fat cells remain in our bodies, empty and dormant. So at any point in our lives, when our intake exceeds our energy consumption, these fat cells start to fill up again. This is the reason why it is so easy to put weight on again once it has been lost. The fat cells are with you for life: this is one of the reasons why diets don't work (see page 218). Once you have been overweight or obese the risk is with you for life, just as is any other medical condition such as diabetes or even high blood pressure. You have to strive to remain on top of it or suffer the consequences.

Chapter 3

What are the consequences of being obese?

There are many consequences of obesity, such as high blood pressure and diabetes but they can be avoided by eating healthily and being active. Those who have these conditions already will find that their health will improve along with a healthy change in lifestyle. A healthy lifestyle started in childhood will go a long way towards helping to prevent your children from developing any of these problems. If you are trying to convince someone that shedding a few pounds or being healthier is important, make them aware of some of the consequences of excess weight.

The consequences of being overweight or obese can be divided into two types of problem – social and health.

Social problems

Western society today does not care for fatness. It is not seen as being attractive or elegant. Research has shown this negative attitude towards fatness since the 1960s. For some people, being overweight or obese simply means that they might find it more difficult to buy clothes or they might find it uncomfortable climbing the stairs at work. For many others, however, the problems can be a lot worse. There are many practical and social examples of how being obese can interfere with the quality of your life. We are bombarded with images of thin, happy, successful people. Many aspire to this image and strive to look like the models and stars they see in fashion magazines and in the films. The bizarre thing is that many of the popular female film stars and pop singers are medically underweight and will suffer health problems such as weak bones and hormonal disorders as a consequence. I find it so sad that people care more about being thin than about being healthy. The reality is that the majority will never look like these underweight 'stars'. Happiness is so often linked to being thin rather than health status. Good examples of this are the eating disorders bulimia and anorexia (which are both on the increase), here the obsession with one's weight and looks overtakes the need to be healthy.

It seems the harder people strive for the ideal body, the more they fail, and are left disappointed and damaged psychologically. A vicious cycle is created with the end-point being lowered

Did you know?

A seven-year study in the US found that 16-year-old girls who were obese left school earlier, were less likely to be married, and had lower earnings than non-obese girls.

Did you know?

Obese children are more likely to be depressed and to go on to become obese adults. It is therefore not surprising that in a study of 40,000 American adults, obese women were 37 per cent more likely to be clinically depressed than healthy-weight women.

self-esteem and confidence. That is why it is so important to use tools such as the BMI and waist circumference to quantify weight objectively. Parents should not comment on their children's appearance and weight but instead promote a healthy weight and active lifestyle. It is much easier to accept one's own body if you know that you are a healthy weight. The aim of this book is not only to improve the foods that your child eats and increase their activity levels but also to improve their confidence and self-esteem.

Childhood is about growing emotionally and psychologically as well as physically. It is the time when the foundation is built for our self-image and our sense of self-worth. The successes and failures experienced during childhood shape your children's character and determination to succeed in their life pursuits, such as careers and in the relationships they build with others.

Children are often extremely honest about their thoughts and feelings. Their small worlds revolve very much around themselves and sometimes they can be insensitive to other children. Much of what children do is influenced by what their friends are doing or what they think their friends would like them to do. The feedback children get from their peers, parents

Did you know?

Obese girls tend to reach puberty before healthy-weight girls. The opposite seems to happen with obese boys, who tend to reach puberty a bit later than healthy-weight boys.

and teachers is extremely important in shaping their self-esteem. Being different in any way can be very difficult for some children. Being an overweight boy who is not great at sports can lead to alienation. A girl who is overweight and cannot fit into the 'right' clothes when all her friends are dressing like the latest girl band can feel isolated.

Obese children are frequently teased and bullied. Name calling can be hurtful and can seriously impact on a child's self-esteem and confidence. Obese children suffer from higher levels of depression than healthy-weight children and, tragically, suicide rates are higher in obese children as well. Studies have also shown that the reverse is true and depressed children and older adults are more likely to become obese. This can spiral out of hand with depression leading to comfort eating leading to weight gain, further depression, more weight gain and so on. This vicious cycle can be very hard to break. If you, or someone you know, is experiencing this problem, seek professional help from your GP or other appropriate health-care professional.

Puberty can be a particularly trying time for girls who go through so many physical changes at this time. As girls tend to reach puberty before boys, they often become very self-conscious of their bodies. There will always be some girls who reach puberty first and this can make matters even worse for them. Avoidance of exercise, combined with an increased appetite owing to rapid growth, can lead to overweight. Excessive weight gained during this time in a young girl's life can prove to be difficult to reverse unless healthy eating and regular exercise become a normal part of life.

The social effects of obesity can have devastating effects. In my case the psychological effects of my weight problem seriously affected my childhood and still linger today even into adulthood. So my aim is to promote healthy lifestyles from as young as five years of age to help families avoid these types of problems. The earlier these problems are dealt with, the better.

Did you know?

The effect of obesity on self-esteem is dependent on a child's age and sex. In girls, the effect of obesity on self-esteem becomes apparent in the pre-teenage years around the age of 9–10. Boys don't seem to be affected until the age of about 13 or 14 when they become more sexually aware.

Did you know?

Self-esteem in adults and children is largely determined by how happy people are with their own physical appearance.

Health problems

According to the World Health Organization, there are four major health concerns associated with being obese:

- Heart disease
- High blood pressure
- Diabetes
- Cancer

Heart disease

The heart is responsible for pumping blood around the body, carrying oxygen to all the cells and removing waste products. Heart attacks are a leading cause of death and for many overweight children the signs of heart disease are already detectable in childhood. A poor diet and insufficient physical activity lead to raised levels of bad fats in the body. These accumulate in the arteries, including those that supply the heart, causing them to narrow. This narrowing can eventually lead to heart disease. If this process starts in childhood, the chance of an early heart attack is more likely.

High blood pressure (hypertension)

The blood that is carried around the body is under pressure in order to keep it moving along our arteries – this is normal. Blood pressure can be measured and is a way of assessing a person's risk of having a heart attack or stroke. Blood pressure tends to rise as we get older. Blood pressure is expressed as two numbers (such as 120/80 or 'one hundred and twenty over

Did you know?

About 80 per cent of obese teenagers have high blood pressure.

eighty'). The higher number is the systolic blood pressure. This is the pressure when your heart is contracted and pumping blood. The lower number is the diastolic blood pressure. This is the pressure when the heart is relaxed and filling with blood. High blood pressure in adults is defined as a systolic blood pressure of 140 or over and/or a diastolic pressure of 90 or over. High blood pressure increases the risk of heart attacks and strokes, kidney damage, eye problems and circulation problems. Obesity is a big risk factor for developing high blood pressure.

Diabetes

Another consequence of the additional weight is the strain it puts on the hormonal system. This may lead to diabetes, the inability by the body to deal with the sugar in our blood, and can cause serious problems such as kidney failure, blindness and gangrene leading to amputation of limbs. There are two types of diabetes. Type I is an autoimmune disorder. It is caused by the immune cells attacking the insulin-producing cells in the pancreas, often following an infection. Type II generally develops over a long period following chronic (long-term) high blood-sugar levels putting a strain on the pancreas and other cells in the body. This used to be called mature-onset diabetes – meaning it developed in older adults – but increasingly it is being diagnosed in young adults and children. Serious problems may develop approximately 10 years after developing the disease. This is bad enough if you are in your 40s or 50s but having such terrible problems in your 20s or 30s is tragic! An eminent researcher has even predicted that obese kids could die from the consequences of their excess weight before their parents.

Case study – diabetes

Michael was 14 years old. He enjoyed most things that boys his age liked. He was not keen on playing sport but he loved to watch football on the television and to be taken by his dad to support the local football team. There was nothing Michael liked more than a curry takeaway and he would also often stop on the way to and from school to stock up on treats to keep him going through the day. Michael's mum cooked every evening and Michael was very fond of her food, with a few exceptions!

Then Michael started developing headaches. They used to come and go but started to affect his school work as he was taking up to five days a month off school. The problem got worse until one day he became so unwell his mum was asked to collect him from school. He was a strange colour, sweating and complaining of a very bad headache and a really sore stomach. Michael's mum rushed him straight to the GP, who immediately sent him to the local hospital for blood tests. The test revealed that Michael had extremely high blood-sugar levels – a sign that he had developed diabetes. Michael was referred to a paediatrician and his mum was shocked to learn that Michael was considered medically obese and that this was a serious risk factor for developing diabetes. I met Michael and his mum and helped them to understand the causes of his excessive weight gain and together we worked on improving his diet in small, manageable ways. We also found a local children's kick-boxing class, which Michael started attending and this has helped to improve his fitness and confidence. He subsequently lost some weight, is managing his diabetes by controlling his diet and does not suffer from headaches any more.

Did you know?

A survey comparing 28,000 obese people to the general population found that the obese men had a 25 per cent increased risk of cancer and obese women a 37 per cent increase risk of cancer.

Cancer

It might come as a surprise but being obese increases your risk of developing cancer. For every type of cancer, more cases are found in obese people than in the general population. An example of this

Did you know?

Every year, 9,000 people in the UK and 50,000 people across the EU die from cancer caused by being overweight or obese. About one-third of all cancers can be prevented by a healthy diet and lifestyle.

is the risk of bowel cancer, which is 2.8 times more common in obese than non-obese people. Cancer rates are not only higher in obese people but also in overweight people. This explains why we are seeing so many more cases of cancer as the number of overweight and obese people increases.

Chapter 4

What are the benefits of a healthy lifestyle?

I have listed some of the more serious illnesses that being obese can lead to but let's now focus on the benefits of being healthy. It is important not to get too hung-up about your weight but rather to judge your health in a broader way by considering the foods you eat and the amount of exercise or physical activity that you do on a regular basis.

Weighing yourself frequently can send the wrong message to your children, who can become obsessed with their own weight on the scales. I usually suggest people weigh themselves every three to six months and not more frequently. A simple way to tell if your body shape or weight is changing is by the feel of your clothes, whether they are looser, tighter or the same.

Case study – crash diets

Becky was a 13-year-old. She loved pop music and one male pop star in particular. Becky and her friends all belonged to his fan group website and were the first to buy his latest music or any magazine with pictures or stories about him. They were dying to see his concert in three months' time and Becky's dad had bought her a ticket for her birthday.

Becky wondered whether he would spot her in the crowd and, like all teenage girls, dreamt of him whisking her off her feet onto the stage and singing a love ballad to her. However, Becky knew this was unlikely to occur and began to blame her figure for that. This led to negative thoughts such as, why would he look at me? I'm so fat, I can't even fit into my favourite pair of jeans. All my friends look better than me, so what chance do I have? Becky spent the night in her room alone crying and did not get much sleep. She decided to follow a diet that she read about in one of her mum's fashion magazines. It involved eating only very small meals during the day and just fruit in the evenings. Because Becky did not want her parents to know that she was dieting she decided to eat fruit during the day and a small meal with her family in the evenings. Her mum thought it great that she was eating so much fruit now and was happy to keep the fruit bowl well stocked. After a few days Becky noticed that she had lost some weight, so she continued the diet, even though she started to feel a little strange. She was really sleepy most of the day and couldn't seem to wake up in the mornings. She was constantly snapping at those around her. Her moods got progressively worse and her parents became concerned about her strange behaviour. Becky was determined to lose weight for the concert and so she persevered. By this stage she was really sick of fruit and switched to eating only vegetables during the day. Becky was now losing weight quite quickly, which was being commented on by those around her. This made her feel good at first. But this was quickly replaced by feelings of depression and exhaustion. Becky got so hungry now that she started raiding the fridge at night. It was on one such night that Becky's dad caught her and realised there was a problem.

I saw Becky and her mum and dad as an urgent private referral. Both parents were very worried. Becky was in tears and confessed to following a fruit and vegetable diet. Her parents were shocked to think that that was all she had been eating during the day and they had not even noticed. I weighed Becky and measured her height and calculated her BMI. Even taking the recent weight loss into account, Becky's BMI just fell in the overweight category, probably due to a recent growth spurt. However, I explained to her that rather than going on a crash diet, a better and healthier approach would be to aim for weight maintenance, while she grows taller. I examined the family's normal diet and discussed with them many practical ways to improve Becky's eating habits. Her parents did not realise that many of the food products they bought were high in sugar and fat. They agreed to support Becky by making the whole family's diet a healthier one. Becky began to eat normally and felt satisfied and full while managing to maintain her weight. The knowledge that she could once again eat safely helped allay her normal teenage concerns and fears. Becky also came to the realisation that if the pop star did decide to like her it would be because of her personality and not her size.

How much and how fast should my child lose weight?

For all growing children, weight loss is not recommended. The recommended approach is to maintain their weight while they get taller – that is, grow into their weight. The Royal College of Paediatrics and Child Health recommend either no weight gain as height increases or weight gain that is slower than height gain. If children go on weight-loss diets, chances are they will not be eating a balanced, varied range of foods and could be at risk of nutritional deficiencies. It is essential that growing children get all the protein, carbohydrate, fat, vitamins, minerals and trace elements their bodies need. By avoiding – or only eating – certain foods, they are likely to miss out on essential nutrients and could face problems later on, such as weak bones, lack of energy or fatigue.

Weight loss is recommended only for children who are under specialist care such as a dietitian, paediatrician or obesity clinic. In these cases, obese children who are over seven years old may benefit from gradual weight loss, say 0.5kg per month. If teenagers have stopped growing, weight loss of around 0.5kg

Crash diets

How many people do you know who have gone on a crash diet and lost weight and managed to keep it off? Most people regain all the lost weight – and put on even more. Don't set yourself or your children up for failure.

per week may be appropriate. Always seek professional advice before encouraging your children to lose weight (see page 263).

The benefits of being a healthy weight can be life-saving. Not falling into the trap of unhealthy eating and the couch-potato lifestyle can mean many more years of health for yourself and your family. All parents want the best for their children. Giving your child the tools necessary for making healthy food choices and the skills to shop for their own food and cook their own meals will be invaluable for the rest of their lives. Making activity and exercise a normal part of their lives and showing them that it can also be fun is a message that will stay with them for life preventing them from becoming yet another statistic. By not putting children on diets and teaching them how to be healthy you are giving them the best present a parent can give their children.

Later on we will look at how to increase the whole family's level of physical activity and at changing unhelpful attitudes and behaviour to helpful ones.

But in the next section we will look at simple and practical steps to improve the family's nutrition and diet.

Part Two

Nutrition and Diet

Chapter 5

Nutrition essentials

Let's start by identifying the different food groups in order to plan your family's meals and to make sure that foods are being eaten in the right proportions. All foods can be put into one of five food groups – **meat and meat alternatives, carbohydrates (starchy foods), milk and dairy products, fruit and vegetables, and fats and sugars.** Many foods are made up of a combination of protein, carbohydrate and fat but are classified according to their most important dietary component. For example, beans contain carbohydrate, protein and a small amount of fat, but their major contribution to our diets is protein and therefore they are classified in the protein group.

Summary of the food groups

- **Meat and meat alternatives:** meat / chicken / turkey / ham / fish / vegetable protein / nuts / eggs / beans / peas / lentils / soya.
- **Carbohydrates (starchy foods):** breads / breakfast cereals /

other cereals such as barley / rye / oats / biscuits / crackers / pasta / rice / potatoes / yams / millet / semolina / rice.

- **Milk and dairy products:** milk / cheese / yoghurt / fromage frais.
- **Fruit and vegetables:** leafy and green vegetables (cabbage, spring greens, kale, cauliflower, Brussels sprouts, broccoli) / root vegetables (carrots, swede, turnips) / salad vegetables (tomatoes, cucumber, lettuce) / mushrooms / sweetcorn / marrows / fruit (apples, bananas, peaches, oranges, melons) / dried fruits and fruit juices.
- **Fats and sugars:** margarine / butter / cooking oils / mayonnaise / cream / salad dressings / chocolates / crisps / savoury snacks / fried foods / gravy / honey / sugary soft drinks / sweets / jam / cakes / puddings / biscuits / pastries.

Test your knowledge of the food groups

For each food, decide which of the five food groups they belong to:

1 - Meat and meat alternatives
2 - Carbohydrates (starchy foods)
3 - Milk and dairy products
4 - Fruits and vegetables
5 - Fats and sugars

Number	Food	Food group - 1/2/3/4 or 5
1.	Fromage frais	
2.	Lentils	
3.	Chicken	
4.	Popcorn	
5.	Cottage cheese	
6.	Beans	
7.	Potatoes	
8.	Butter	
9.	Boiled sweets	
10.	Minced beef	
11.	Jelly beans	
12.	Pure fruit juice	
13.	Muffin	
14.	Nuts	
15.	Ice cream	
16.	Bread	
17.	Sugary soft drink	
18.	Rice cakes	

Answers:

1. Fromage frais is made from cow's milk and therefore belongs in the **milk and dairy products food group.**
2. Lentils are part of the **meat and meat alternatives group** as they are a useful source of protein, especially for vegetarians.
3. Chicken, as with all animal meats, is part of the **meat and meat alternatives group.**
4. Popcorn is very high in carbohydrate and therefore part of the **carbohydrate, or starchy foods, group.**
5. Cottage cheese is made from cow's milk and therefore part of the **milk and dairy products group.**
6. Beans contain carbohydrate but their major contribution to the diet is their high content of protein and therefore they belong to the **meat and meat alternatives group.**
7. Potatoes are often misclassified as a vegetable, whereas in fact they consist mainly of carbohydrate and therefore are placed in the **carbohydrate, or starchy foods, group.**
8. Butter is made from cow's milk but consists predominantly of fat therefore placing it in the **fat and sugars group.**
9. Boiled sweets consist predominantly of sugar and therefore fall in **fats and sugars group.**
10. Minced beef belongs in the **meat and meat alternatives group.**
11. Jelly beans consist mainly of sugar and therefore belong in the **fats and sugars group.**

12. Pure fruit juice is high in fruit sugar, or fructose, but also contains vitamins and minerals and so it belongs in **the fruit and vegetables group**. Note: only one glass a day counts towards the recommended five daily portions of fruit and vegetables.
13. Muffins are mostly flour and so although they contain fat, are predominantly carbohydrate and therefore part of the **carbohydrate, or starchy foods, group**.
14. Nuts are a good source of protein and therefore part of the **meat and meat alternatives group**.
15. Ice cream is made from cow's milk and therefore belongs in the **milk and dairy product group**.
16. Bread is made from flour, which is mainly carbohydrate, and therefore part of the **carbohydrate, or starchy foods, group**.
17. Sugary soft drinks contain sugar and not much else, and so are part of the **fats and sugars group**.
18. Rice cakes are made from rice which is high in carbohydrate and so part of the **carbohydrate, or starchy foods, group**.

Now that you know the different food groups we are going to use them as the basis for explaining how to improve your family's diet. The nutrition guidelines in this book are based on low-Glycaemic Index (GI) eating combined with low-fat healthy eating to promote long-term good health and optimal weight control for the future.

Chapter 6

The Glycaemic Index (GI)

GI is not just another weight-loss diet designed by crackpot doctors or nutritionists or Hollywood diet gurus but rather a scientifically proven method of categorising foods. The method is designed to help you maintain stable blood-sugar levels and keep you feeling fuller for longer. GI is not new, and in fact has been around for a while. It was developed initially to help diabetics control their blood-sugar levels. More recently, the general health-promoting benefits of GI have come to light. Following a healthy GI way of eating has many health benefits. It promotes a healthy heart, prevents diabetes (as well as helps control it) and can also aid in weight loss or maintenance – without you having to starve yourself! GI is used in some hospitals to treat overweight adults and children. Best of all it is a great way for the general population to eat healthily.

Research has shown that low-GI foods, or 'slow-release foods', take longer to be digested in the gut and absorbed into the bloodstream. This promotes a feeling of fullness for longer periods of time, making it less likely you'll want to overeat. In contrast, high-GI foods or 'fast-release foods', are digested and absorbed too quickly. This causes rapid swings in blood-sugar levels, leaving you feeling tired and hungry soon after eating. Unfortunately, the average Western diet is generally full of high-GI (fast-release) foods. Many of the products found on our supermarket shelves are highly processed and filled with ingredients that are very quickly digested and absorbed into our bloodstream such as sugar and starch fillers. Low-GI foods are better for us than refined, processed ones, which not only have a high-GI score but are also often full of unhealthy fats and salt.

GI makes healthy eating simple to do as it breaks foods down into three groups – low, medium and high – depending on their GI score. This categorisation is based on studies that measure the rate at which foods are digested and absorbed as glucose (a type of sugar) into the bloodstream. Some foods are digested extremely quickly and then absorbed rapidly into the bloodstream, examples being white bread, sugar, potatoes – all considered to be high GI or fast release. Other foods are broken down more slowly. For example, spaghetti, multigrain bread and muesli are classified as low GI or slow release. There is another category, known as medium GI, that falls between low and high GI. This difference in the speed that these foods are converted into the glucose in our bloodstream is the basis of the GI system. For overall health and wellbeing, we should have more foods that have a low-GI rating.

GI scores range from 0–100 with water, 0, being the lowest GI and glucose, 100, one of the highest.

Glycaemic Index (GI)

Using GI can help to stabilise blood sugar levels, reduce the risk of diseases such as diabetes and heart disease and help prevent excessive weight gain. It is scientifically proven that foods with a low GI are more filling than foods with a high GI.

Low GI = Slow release = Healthy foods

High GI = Fast release = Unhealthy foods

It is possible to lower the overall GI of a meal by mixing low-GI foods with high-GI products. For example, eating jacket potatoes (high GI) topped with baked beans (low GI) and served with a side salad (low GI) will make the overall GI of the meal lower than if the potatoes were eaten on their own. It is also possible to lower the GI of a higher GI food by eating it with protein and adding vinegar or lemon juice.

Low GI, high fat

It is important to be aware of foods that are low GI and high fat, especially those high in unhealthy fats (see page 78). In order to be healthy and control your weight, high-fat foods, although low GI, should also be avoided or limited in the diet. An example is thin and crispy pizza, which is low GI but, owing to the cheese and meat toppings, can be very high in saturated fat. Therefore just based on its GI it would seem acceptable, but it is not something that should be eaten on a regular basis (see page 82 for a list of low-GI, high-fat foods to be avoided).

Our ancestors' diets

In ancient times, and especially before modern-day technology and food processing methods were invented, food was prepared quite differently from the way it is today. Crops were planted and harvested by hand, and grains prepared by grinding or crushing, using stones, mortar and pestle, or cooking for a very long time. Generally, the whole grain was eaten, including the fibrous outer layers, which contain most of the fibre, vitamins and minerals. Preparing foods was a long, hard process and the food our ancestors ate was heavier and denser and so had to be chewed for longer and took longer to digest. This meant they felt full for longer periods. These foods are now known as low-GI or 'unrefined' foods. Compare this to the way we eat today. We can easily buy food from many places that requires little or

Refined and unrefined foods

Refined	Unrefined
white rice	brown rice
white flour	wholegrain flour
white bread	multigrain or granary bread
white pasta	wholemeal pasta
biscuits	wholemeal muffin
cakes	flapjacks
refined breakfast cereals (Rice Krispies, Coco Pops, Frosties)	unrefined breakfast cereals (oat porridge, All Bran, natural muesli)

An activity for the whole family

Rub the following refined and unrefined foods between your hands and chew a small piece in your mouth to compare them: brown rice and white rice, wholegrain flour and white flour, wholegrain/granary bread and white bread. The white foods have had a lot of their goodness removed and the brown or grainy foods are packed full of vitamins, fibre and minerals and so are far healthier and give longer-lasting energy. The unrefined foods take a lot longer to chew and leave you feeling fuller and more satisfied.

no preparation and very little chewing and digestion, owing to the fact that it is so refined that most of the nutritious fibrous outer layers have been removed from the grains. These foods are high GI or 'refined' foods. Many of these foods have added ingredients such as fats or sugars that add unnecessary energy. So not only is the food digested more quickly, leading to a quick return to feeling hungry again, but if it exceeds our daily energy requirements it is stored as fat.

What happens to our sugar levels when we eat high-GI foods?

When we eat foods that have a high-GI score, they are quickly digested and absorbed into the bloodstream. This rapid rise in blood glucose causes the body to release insulin (a hormone) from the pancreas. Insulin causes the glucose in the blood to be absorbed by the cells and used as energy, with any excess being stored as fat in our fat cells. Once the glucose has moved into the cells, the levels in the blood drop and we feel hungry again, causing us to want to eat more food. In certain people, this can lead to rapid swings between high and low blood sugar, which causes them to feel tired and hungry, to crave more food than they need and to put on excess weight. Having high levels of insulin due to a high-GI diet is not a good thing as insulin causes the body to store fat continually. This makes it very difficult to break down fat stores and lose weight. A diet full of high-GI foods can put excess strain on the pancreas as it is forced to produce more and more insulin. This can eventually lead to the development of diabetes.

What happens to our sugar levels when we eat low-GI foods?

When we eat foods with a low-GI score, the food is digested and absorbed more slowly into the bloodstream. This slow rise in glucose leads to a slow release of insulin, which allows the body time to think where it needs to send the sugar to be used for energy, and not stored as fat. Because smaller amounts of insulin are released, blood sugar does not drop so fast and so we feel more satisfied and less hungry. This feeling of fullness leads to less snacking and helps prevent excess weight gain.

Good reasons to eat low-GI foods

- Low-GI foods protect your heart by reducing blood levels of triglyceride (a type of fat that can lead to narrowing of the

The science of measuring the GI of a food.

Measuring the GI of foods is a lengthy process, performed in a laboratory by scientists. Human volunteers are asked to eat different types of food, all containing exactly 50 grams of carbohydrate. A sample of their blood is then taken every 15-30 minutes for two hours and their blood sugar measured. The blood-sugar levels are then plotted on a computer graph and compared to the same volunteers' response to 50g of glucose. This gives the GI of these foods for each person. The GI of the food is the average value taken from eight to ten volunteers. Not all foods have been measured as the whole process is expensive and time-consuming, but more foods are being added to the list all the time.

arteries) and increasing blood levels of good cholesterol (which protects the heart).

- Low-GI foods are less refined and so tend to be higher in fibre. Fibre is an important element of the diet. It aids healthy bowel functioning and reduces the risk of certain colon and other digestive cancers.
- Dermatologists claim that eating lots of sugary foods can lead to high levels of highly damaging molecules called free radicals in our skin, which lead to wrinkles and poor skin tone.
- Want more energy when exercising? Eat low-GI foods as they produce longer-lasting energy to fuel our muscles.

- Low-GI foods provide steady energy levels for the brain and can improve attention span and memory.
- Risk of developing diabetes can be reduced by switching to a low-GI diet.
- If you already suffer from diabetes, then keeping to a low-GI diet will help stabilise your blood-glucose levels.

Case study – high GI diet

Clare is an eleven-year-old girl who lives with her mother during the week, as her parents have separated, and spends weekends with her dad and his new wife. Clare loves visiting her dad as there are always plenty of treats around and his new wife, who works in a supermarket, gives her loads of sweets and crisps to take home with her for the rest of the week. Clare hides these, as she knows her mum would not approve. She is always going on about being healthy and not eating too many treats.

Clare's mum works a very long day and generally leaves very early in the mornings. She always tells her daughter to eat breakfast, but Clare is usually running late so breakfast is the last thing she worries about. On the way to school she stops at the corner shop and spends most of her day's pocket money on sweets and crisps. By the time the first lesson begins, she feels ravenous and can barely concentrate on what is being taught. She begins to suck and chew her way through her entire lolly bag and packet of crisps. Often her teachers catch her and sometimes give her detention or ask her to leave the classroom, as her sucking and chewing sounds and hyperactive behaviour is disruptive. Clare does not bring her own lunch to school and looks forward to school dinners, which, for her usually consist of a choice of pizza, burger, fish fingers or chicken nuggets and chips, followed by a sugary pudding. By mid-afternoon Clare often feels weak and dizzy. One day when her dizziness and weakness were unusually severe, she was sent to the school nurse who enquired about her diet. When Clare told her how she eats sweets instead of a normal breakfast and described the food choices she usually made at the school canteen, the nurse decided to involve her mother. Clare's mum was asked to attend a meeting with the head teacher. At the meeting, the head teacher explained that Clare's behaviour was erratic, restless, loud and disruptive and constantly complained of weakness and dizziness. Clare's mum was shocked as this did not sound like her daughter at all. The head teacher suggested that Clare's behaviour could be related to the foods she was eating and asked her mum to look into this.

Clare's mum arranged to see me for a dietary review. I met with Clare and her mum, where we discussed Clare's food intake during the week and at the weekends. After analysing the full diet, I came to the conclusion that skipping breakfast and then eating lots of high-GI foods could be causing Clare's mood swings. Her lack of energy followed by periods of hyperactivity, dizziness and weakness could be a sign of fluctuating blood-sugar levels. The first step was to make sure that Clare ate breakfast every morning, and that the treats came to a stop (except occasionally after meals – under supervision) and that the school catering staff made sure that she had fruit instead of a rich pudding and did not eat chips every day. We also agreed that her mum provided a sandwich and pieces of fruit for Clare to eat at home or on the way to school.

A month later, Clare's mum met with the head teacher again who was delighted to say that there have been no complaints from Clare's teachers. The dinner ladies said that Clare gets a bit upset when they refuse to serve her pudding and chips but overall she has begun to eat more vegetables and fruit. By cutting out some of the high-GI snacks and foods in Clare's diet, her behaviour and health have been improved significantly.

Chapter 7

Food groups and GI

Popular foods that have had their GI measured are listed in the table of GI values (see page 165) but here are some general rules to help you decide if a food is low, medium or high GI.

Meat and meat alternatives

Chicken, fish, meat and vegetable protein are generally low GI but can have a higher GI if they are they are covered in batter or served with other refined carbohydrates, for example, fish or chicken fried in batter, or a burger in a white bread bun served with dips.

Carbohydrates (starchy foods)

Bread, rice and pasta can be low or high GI, depending on how refined they are – white bread or granary bread for example – and whether high-GI additives have been included – such as sugars and refined starches – so always read the labels.

Examples of high-GI additives include table sugar (sucrose), dextrose, glucose, malt, syrup, maltodextrin, maltose, treacle and hydrolysed starch. Most old or white potatoes are high GI and best avoided. However, new potatoes and sweet potatoes are medium GI and can be eaten in moderation.

Milk and dairy products

These are low GI, but full-fat versions contain animal fat, which is bad for the heart. Ice cream is a low-GI food but high in unhealthy fat therefore it is categorised as a low-GI/high-fat food. It is recommended that you switch from full-cream, full-fat dairy products to low-fat or fat-free versions. For example, replace full-cream milk with skimmed milk. Choose low-fat cottage cheese and low-fat yoghurt or try natural fat-free yoghurts and add your own fruit combination.

Fruit and vegetables

Eat a minimum of five portions of fruit and vegetables per day. Most fruit are low GI, but some are medium and some high GI. Since fruit is important for the diet and a good source of vitamins, minerals and fibre, do not worry about the GI of fruit too much but try to avoid eating the high-GI fruits such as dried dates, ripe bananas and watermelon too often.

How much is a portion of fruit and veg?

Each of the following is a portion of fruit and veg:

- One whole medium-sized fruit or vegetable, such as an apple, orange or banana.
- A couple of small fruits, such as plums, or a cupful of very small fruits, such as grapes or berries.
- Half to one tablespoon of dried fruits such as raisins, prunes or apricots.
- A piece of a large fruit such as half a grapefruit, a wedge of melon, a couple of rings of pineapple, half an avocado.
- Two tablespoons of raw, cooked, frozen or canned vegetables.
- A bowl of salad.
- A glass of fruit juice (200ml) – this only counts **once** per day.
- **Don't** count a glass of squash, an artificial 'fruit flavoured' drink, fruit yoghurt, fruit and nut chocolate or a tablespoon of jam – there is not enough fruit in them to make one portion.

Easy ways to get your kids to eat their five servings a day!

- Smoothies: Give your children a healthy start with a filling fruit smoothie. All you need is a blender, fresh or frozen fruit, ice, and optional ingredients such as low-fat milk, low-fat yoghurt, low-fat ice cream or low-fat soya milk.
- Fresh fruit platters: A selection of your children's favourite fruits arranged in a fun and creative design can tempt even the most unwilling. Try topping with your favourite low-fat dairy product, such as low-fat cottage cheese, or low-fat yoghurt. Serve as a dessert with low-fat ice cream or custard.

- Porridge and cereals: Liven up your children's breakfast cereal choice with a handful of raisins, or fresh, chopped apples, pears or prunes.
- Frozen fruit lollipops: Blend a piece of fruit with a tub of low-fat yoghurt or semi-skimmed milk. Add a tablespoon of apple purée (see below) or 50ml of pure fruit juice. Place in a lolly-shaped container and freeze. No child can refuse. Be sure to use their favourite fruits. Try adding some crazy food colourings to make them more fun.
- Poached fruit: Poach some fruit in a saucepan with a little water and serve with a scoop of low-fat ice cream or yoghurt to make an inviting dessert for the whole family. It can also be served on its own, in cereal on hot porridge or with a slice of French toast (made with low-GI bread).
- Barbecued bananas: Place a banana on the barbecue for a simple dessert, or try slicing it open, wrapping it in foil and placing under the grill. It is a hit with everyone. Try spreading some light cream cheese, cinnamon and a sprinkle of almonds in the middle for an extra special touch. Also try experimenting with a pineapple, pear or apple.
- Home-made apple purée spread: Take some apples and core, peel and cut into chunks. Add a handful of raisins or dates and 120ml of pure apple juice, bring to the boil and simmer until cooked. Spice it up with a splash of lemon juice and ginger. Use to sweeten your favourite foods or eat straight from a bowl. It is delicious as a spread on toast instead of jam.
- Fruity pancakes: Use fruit as a topping on home-cooked low-GI oaty pancakes (see page 134) or crêpes. Alternatively,

chop the fruit into pancake batter mixture and create exotic, tantalising fruity pancakes. Additional fruit can be added on top. Tasty combos can include dried, fresh or frozen fruits such as berries, bananas and figs with fat-free fromage frais and a dash of jam or honey.

- Apricot nut bread: Do you enjoy baking your own bread? If so, why not add in dried apricots, raisins or fresh bananas and nuts for a nutty fruit bread delight. The whole family will enjoy it.
- Yoghurt surprise: Mix 100ml pineapple juice into natural low-fat yoghurt and one teaspoon of vanilla essence and sweeten to taste with artificial sweetener, or add some apple purée instead. Grate a fresh pear into the combination and add some chopped nuts, dried fruit and one tablespoon of unsweetened muesli.
- Chop some fresh, crunchy vegetables into bite-size pieces and serve with a variety of tasty dips such as hummus, low-fat cheese spread, salsa (beware of added sugar) and tzatziki (yoghurt and cucumber dip).
- Slice a banana and add to your child's favourite low-GI cereal.
- Mash banana on low-GI toast with some cinnamon. Avoid using butter or margarine as it adds unnecessary fat.
- For a healthy, quick snack, grill some cheese and tomato on a slice of granary/wholegrain bread or wholemeal pitta bread.
- Include a piece of fruit in your child's packed lunch, or chopped fruit served with yoghurt or fruit juice in a pot with a tight-fitting lid.

- Cook different coloured vegetables, such as cauliflower, peas or butternut, and mash to make a tasty purée to serve with meals.
- Stir-fry vegetables with some meat, fish or chicken to make a tempting Chinese-style meal.
- Add sliced or puréed vegetables to pasta sauces, soups, casseroles or stews.
- Serve canned fruit (in natural fruit juice – not syrup) with a yoghurt as a tasty dessert or snack.
- Leave a plate of chopped fruit at eye-level in your fridge to tempt them when they are foraging through the fridge for a snack.

Fats

Fats are low GI but this does not mean that they are all healthy. Fat is the highest source of calories in the diet, providing nine calories per gram compared to four calories per gram from carbohydrate and protein. The four different types of fat all have different effects on our health. They are: saturated, polyunsaturated, monounsaturated and trans (or hydrogenated) fats.

Saturated fat

This nearly always comes from an animal and is the main dietary cause of high cholesterol and heart disease. It is found in full-fat dairy products (cheese, cream, ice cream, yoghurts), meat (burgers, chicken, lamb, steak, pork chops, hot dogs) and butter or dairy spreads (sandwich spreads). Coconut oil and palm oil are also high in saturated fat. They are cheap to use and a favourite ingredient in store-bought snack foods, such as crisps and biscuits. Always check the labels and ensure that you buy foods containing less than 5g of saturated fat per 100g.

Monounsaturated fat

This is a good cholesterol-free fat and can help lower harmful cholesterol levels and keep your heart healthy and strong. This fat is found in olives, almonds, peanuts, avocados, seeds (such as sunflower seeds and sesame seeds), nuts (such as almonds, peanuts and hazelnuts), rapeseed oil, canola oil and olive oil. Use these oils for cooking and salad dressings. The Mediterranean diet, as eaten in France, Italy and Spain, uses mostly olive oil in cooking and salad dressings. These countries have some of the lowest rates of heart disease in the world.

Polyunsaturated fat

This is another, health-promoting, cholesterol-free fat. It is commonly found in vegetable oils (sunflower, cornflower and flaxseed). The most beneficial form is omega-3 fats. It is found in oily fish, such as salmon, mackerel, sardines, pilchards and fresh tuna, rapeseed oil, walnut oil and flaxseed oil. This fat is essential for adults and growing children and it is recommended that oily fish (baked or grilled) should be eaten 2–4 times per week. Note: pregnant and breastfeeding women and girls under 16 should not eat more than 2 portions per week (a portion = 140g). For more information see www.food.gov.uk

Trans (hydrogenated) fats

These are the unhealthiest of the fats and should be avoided where possible. They are processed vegetable oils that have been heat-treated and chemically altered to make them thicker. This converts them into high-cholesterol fats, which cause thickening of the arteries contributing to heart attack and stroke. They are found in hard margarines, cereals, baked foods (biscuits, cakes, and doughnuts), fast foods, fried foods and snack foods.

Simple ways to reduce the amount of unhealthy fats in your diet

As fat is high in calories it can lead to excess weight gain. It is especially important to reduce the unhealthy fats, in order to promote good health and wellbeing.

- Replace all full-cream dairy products with low-fat or fat-free alternatives, such as semi-skimmed milk, low-fat or fat-free yoghurt, low-fat cottage cheese (most white cheeses are naturally lower in fat than yellow cheeses).
- Use evaporated skimmed milk instead of cream when preparing sauces or soups for your family.
- Fat-free natural yoghurt or fat-free fromage frais can replace sour cream in recipes. You can also use skimmed milk mozzarella instead of cheddar cheese.
- Use tomato-based pasta sauces instead of creamy ones.
- Avoid fried foods or foods in batter. Instead try steamed, boiled, baked or grilled foods.
- Look out for low-fat sandwich spreads and light salad dressing to add flavour.

- Try cooking with low-calorie cooking sprays and use non-stick frying pans. This will allow you to reduce the amount of oil used when cooking.
- Avoid baked products such as doughnuts, cakes and flap-jacks as they often contain high levels of fat.
- Wholegrain and unrefined starches are generally low in fat, it is what you spread on them that makes the difference – so avoid butter or high-fat spreads.
- Porridge oats are a good choice for breakfasts; avoid granola cereals or rich mueslis as they are usually high in fat.
- Remove the skin from chicken or turkey before cooking, as it contains most of the saturated fat.
- Baking, roasting and grilling are the healthiest ways to prepare meat.
- Always choose lean cuts of meat.
- Chicken, ham or turkey slices are generally healthy low-fat choices.
- White meats, such as chicken, turkey and ham are lower in fat than dark meats, such as beef, lamb or duck.
- Fish should be baked, grilled or steamed to bring out their natural flavours. Avoid pub-style battered, fried fish.
- Occasional desserts can be part of a healthy diet. Look for low-fat chocolate mousse or puddings at your local supermarket.
- Beans and other pulses are low in fat, high in protein, nutritious and tasty. For a change, try lentils, chickpeas and soya beans instead of meat in casseroles and stews, or buy textured vegetable protein (TVP) products such as Quorn – or soya-based sausages and burgers.

- Avoid fried snacks such as potato crisps. Instead try hot-air popped popcorn, or baked corn, or wheat tortilla chips.
- Try low-fat ice cream or low-fat frozen yoghurt instead of full-cream ice cream.
- As a treat, serve low-fat custard on its own, poured over chopped fruit or sugar-free jelly.

Choose your fats wisely

Foods such as avocados, salmon and nuts contain fats that are super healthy and help fight heart disease.

- All fats, even healthy ones need to be eaten in moderation because they have twice as many calories as protein and starch and can lead to excess weight gain.
- Unhealthy fats are easy to recognise – they almost always

Low-GI/high-unhealthy-fat foods – to be avoided

Some foods are low GI but high in unhealthy fat and so should be avoided or restricted in the diet. They include butter, hard margarine, cream, lard, ghee, full-fat cheese (such as parmesan or feta) and full-fat yoghurt, ice cream, cream-based soups and sauces, fried fish fingers, pork chops, ribs, sausages, lamb, hot dogs, chicken nuggets, fried bacon, pizza, coconut milk, coconut oil, palm oil, chocolates, fried dumplings and spring rolls, crispy duck, meat lasagne, cream-covered or cheese filled raviolis, taramasalata, high-fat dressings, mayonnaise, caesar salads and coleslaw.

come from an animal source and are solid at room temperature – lard and butter, for example.

- Always read labels to identify the amount and type of fat present (see page 89).

Sugar

Sugar is often referred to as 'empty calories' providing energy but no vitamins, minerals or fibre. There are four main types of sugar in the diet and not all are bad for us!

Glucose

Glucose is highly refined and has a GI score of 100. It is often added to sweets and high energy sports drinks. Foods with added glucose should be avoided unless you are an elite athlete and need a quick energy fix.

Sucrose

Sucrose is another name for the common white table sugar that we add to our tea and cereals. It is high GI and also highly refined and provides no nutritional benefits. Sucrose should be avoided.

Fructose

Fructose is a natural sugar found in fruit. Fructose in fruit is low GI. When we eat a piece of fruit, the fructose we absorb has not been refined and therefore has a lower GI score, which makes it healthier than glucose and sucrose. However, sometimes manufacturers extract fructose from fruit and refine it from corn or from sugar cane and sugar beet using a chemical process. It is then used to sweeten other foods, such as fruit juices or yoghurts. This sweetens food and increases its energy but provides no additional nutritional benefits. A common food additive is high-fructose corn syrup, which some researchers believe is contributing to the rapid rise in obesity in the USA and should be avoided if possible.

Lactose

Lactose is a naturally occurring sugar found in milk and dairy products. It is low GI. Lactose is not a problem in the diet and has no negative effects in most people. However some people may suffer food intolerance to lactose and should avoid it.

What should my child drink?

Fruit juice contains lots of sugar. You need to squeeze four or five oranges to make one glass of fresh orange juice. It is much better to eat the whole fruit as you will be getting all the fibre

Foods and drinks to avoid:

- Sugary soft-drinks and sports drinks (high GI, high sugar)
- Sweets (high GI, high sugar)
- Chips/crisps (high GI, high fat)
- Highly refined and sugary breakfast cereals such as Coco-Pops, corn flakes, Frosties, Rice Krispies (high GI and/or high sugar)

and it will make you feel fuller for longer. Only have one glass of fruit juice per day. The best drinks for children are skimmed (fat-free), or semi-skimmed (low-fat) milk and water. Sugar-free fizzy drinks can be included in the diet but in moderate amounts as they can increase dental caries due to their acidity.

How much should my child drink?

Children should aim to drink 6–8 glasses of fluid per day. If their wee is dark yellow then they need to drink more – it should be a very light yellow, like straw. If they are exercising it is important to drink plenty to avoid becoming dehydrated.

Artificial sweeteners

Artificial sweeteners are used in foods and drinks as an alternative to sugar. They are intensely sweet and so you need very little to give the same sweetness as sugar. Their benefit is that they are very low in calories. Foods labelled 'no added sugar' often contain artificial sweeteners and it is wise to read labels so you are aware of the ingredients. There has been a lot of misinformation on the dangers of artificial sweeteners. Many studies have shown most to be safe for the majority of people. One exception is cyclamate. The Foods Standards Agency, as a precautionary measure, advises parents to give young children aged one to four years no more than three glasses a day of squash containing this artificial sweetener. In most cases, children drinking large amounts of squash containing aspartame, acesulfame K, saccharin or sucralose would not exceed the safe limits for these sweeteners. However, as a precaution, as children are still growing, it is probably wise not to allow the consumption of excessive amounts daily of foods and drinks containing artificial sweeteners. Aspartame is broken down to phenylalanine in the body – a risk to children suffering from phenylketonuria, a metabolic disorder.

So what are the benefits and why do I recommend the use of artificial sweeteners in my recipes? The main reason is that artificial sweeteners do not affect blood sugar levels and do not add excessive calories to many foods that children love to eat. The sugar levels in foods commonly eaten are at a record high. This contributes excessive calories to the diet and over time can lead to excessive weight gain. Table sugar (sucrose) is high GI therefore any food or drink that has added sugar will have a higher GI than if no sugar was added at all. Glucose, too is high GI and is often added to sports drinks. Since children's diets are already so high in sugar, they have developed a strong 'taste' for sweetness, which can be hard to break, in my experience. A general complaint from children who are overweight and who follow my healthy-eating guidelines or go on weight-loss diets is that their desserts, breakfast cereals and drinks are not sweet enough. This can often cause them to abandon the healthy foods and drinks in favour of the sugary, sweet versions that led to the problem in the first place. So I allow the use of artificial sweeteners in breakfast cereals, desserts and drinks for children in the early stages of my eating plan. But I recommend that parents gradually decrease the amounts they use in order to wean their children off these products. If this is done steadily, you can decrease a child's affinity for sweet foods. Foods that are naturally sweet, such as oranges, grapes and pineapple, can be offered when a child has a craving for sweetness, especially after meals and for a snack. Some parents refuse to use artificial sweeteners because they dislike the taste, although the newest sweetener, sucralose is made from sugar and has a similar taste to sugar but with fewer calories. If parents are strongly adverse to artificial sweeteners, I recommend that a small amount of honey can be used to sweeten foods and in baking. Honey is medium GI and therefore has a better effect on blood-sugar levels than table sugar. In my recipes (see page 131), I have tried to give you a choice of artificial sweetener or honey, so feel free to use whichever you prefer.

Salt

Salt is made up of sodium and chloride. It's the sodium in salt that can be bad for your health. In the old days, when food was natural and not full of refined ingredients, people did not have to worry too much about the amount of salt they ate. Today, manufacturers add salt to nearly all processed products, including meats, breakfast cereals, biscuits, sausages, cheese, canned and instant soups, ready prepared meals, takeaway food, crisps, nuts and even baked beans.

So why are we worried?

Salt – or the sodium it contains – is linked to high blood pressure which is a contributing factor to heart disease and stroke. So it is important to watch out for products that contain excess amounts of it.

How much salt do we need?

Adults need less than 6g of salt per day. For children, see below:

- 4 to 6 years – 3g salt a day (1.2g sodium)
- 7 to 10 years – 5g salt a day (2g sodium)
- 11 and over – 6g salt a day (2.4g sodium)

How do I convert sodium into salt?

Sodium is usually listed in the nutritional information on food labels. Salt is also listed on some foods, but not all. If you know how much sodium is in a particular food, you can work out roughly the amount of salt that it contains by multiplying the sodium by 2.5. So if a portion of food contains 1.2g sodium then it contains about 3g salt.

So how do I reduce the salt in my family's diet?

- In order to avoid complaints that your food needs more salt, gradually reduce the amount you use in home-cooked foods so that your family's taste buds can adapt slowly.
- If necessary, add a bit of salt while cooking but do not put a salt cellar on the table. That way you are in control of the salt intake of your family.
- Experiment with different spices and herbs to add flavour to your meals.
- Buy products such as reduced-salt soya sauce and baked beans with lower levels.
- Avoid very salty products such as packet soups and sauces.

For more information on salt in the diet, see www.salt.gov.uk

Chapter 8

Reading labels

Always read food labels to decide if the product belongs in your trolley. By law, there must be two sources of information on all products (except fresh fruit and vegetables and bakery products). The first is the added ingredients list, which must show all the constituents in the product (except those present in very small amounts). The second is the nutritional information table. Use both to ensure no unhealthy products get into your kitchen by accident.

Ingredients list

This shows all ingredients used to produce a food or drink. By law, all ingredients must be listed in descending order of quantity. Often the main ingredients will have a percentage in brackets to tell you how much is present – for example: spaghetti bolognese, beef (23%). This allows you to compare products. For example, there is a huge variety of sausages available and it is well worth taking time to find the product with the highest amount of meat. The higher the percentage of beef or pork, the lower the proportion of filler material. If sugar or fat comes near the top of the list of ingredients you know immediately that the food is probably worth avoiding. Look out for the other names of refined starches or sugars, such as sucrose, syrup, dextrose, and hydrolysed starch.

Nutrition information table

Always look at the 'per 100g' (gram) column as the 'per serving' column is not very useful for comparing foods. You will then be able to choose the healthiest varieties. This will initially make shopping a longer process but in a short time you will become familiar with the healthier brands, boosting your family's health. Let's take a look at an example of a nutrition label:

Nutrition information	Typical values per 100g
Energy	**389Kj (kilojoules)/58Kcal (calories)**
Protein	**4.6g**
Carbohydrate	**7.2g**
of which sugars	6.6g
Fat	**1.2g**
of which saturates	0.3g
Fibre	**0.3g**
Sodium	**0.2g**

The nutrition label above tells you that there are 58 calories (we use calories in the UK) per 100g of the product. There is also

4.6g per 100g of protein and 7.2g of carbohydrate. The important part is how much sugar is present? In this product, 6.6g of the total 7.2g of carbohydrate is actual sugar. I consider anything above 5g per 100g to be high and I recommend avoiding these most of the time. It is important to remember that there are a couple of exceptions – when the food is a dairy product or contains fruit, the sugars will be high but are lactose and fructose, which do not have to be avoided in their natural forms. By looking at the added ingredients, you will be able to tell if sugars or modified starches have been added and then by reading the nutrition label you can see how much is present.

This product has 1.2g of fat per 100g and a small amount of this is saturated fat. Remember to avoid foods high in fat (generally above 5–10g per 100g). Fibre helps our bowels to work properly and this product contains a small amount (0.3g per 100g). Last but not least is sodium which is found in salt. The sodium level on its own does not tell us much and should be converted to salt by multiplying by 2.5. For example, this

Did you know?

The Food Standards Agency is working with food manufacturers and other organisations and experts to develop a nutrient profiling system to make it easy for people to tell whether a food is healthy or not, just by looking at a diagram. The specially developed system will be on the front of food labels so that you can easily check whether the food is suitable for your family.

product contains 0.2g of sodium which is equivalent to 0.5g of salt. Remember to then multiply by the amount that is eaten. For example, if you ate 200g of this product, you would have consumed 1.0g of salt.

Chapter 9

So how do I improve my family's diet?

Low-GI eating is not a diet that you follow for a short period to lose weight. A low-GI eating plan is for life. The aim is to include as many low-GI foods as possible while reducing the high-GI ones. Children are growing and so you should not restrict the amounts of food they are eating, simply ensure that they are eating low-GI foods and that you are providing a balanced diet. Children also need healthy snacks between meals. By eating low-GI foods, they are more likely to stay full longer, thereby decreasing the risk of unnecessary unhealthy snacking. If your child is overweight, keep an eye on portion sizes (see page 125) but rest assured that it is very difficult to gain excess weight on a low-GI eating plan. In fact, combined with the recommended amounts of physical activity, it will contribute to a gradual stabilisation of weight and possibly even some weight loss.

Healthy eating tips

- Choose low-GI foods and ingredients for home-cooked meals.
- Choose healthy fats over unhealthy ones.
- Eat five servings of fruit and vegetables per day.
- Unrefined, unprocessed foods are best.
- Breakfast is the most important meal of the day.
- High-GI snacks are quick-fix foods and can leave you feeling tired and moody.
- Always eat three meals a day and at least two healthy snacks.
- Eating low-GI is not a diet but a way to make the most of the food you do eat.

What should I stock in my kitchen?

Removing unhealthy temptations from the kitchen reduces the likelihood of your child snacking on inappropriate food. It is not

STOP!

1. Piling up your child's plate with food.
2. Serving rich puddings after every meal.
3. Leaving unhealthy snacks and junk food lying around.
4. Eating separately from your children.
5. Allowing the family to eat in front of the television.

START!

1. Serving the recommended portion sizes (see page 125).
2. Saving puddings for special occasions - at other times offer fruit to finish off your family meals.
3. Stocking up on healthy low-GI snacks to help your family avoid temptation.
4. Eating your main meal together, as a family.
5. Serving food at the dinner/kitchen table only.
6. Spending more time with your children being active - especially in the evenings and at weekends.

fair to expect your child to avoid temptations such as biscuits, chocolates and crisps if they are left lying about or easily accessible in kitchen cupboards (children are very curious and it won't take long for them to find your secret stash). The key to successful eating at home is to replace unhealthy, inappropriate foods with wholesome appropriate ones. Shelves should be stocked with healthy foods only. You do not have to throw unhealthy food away but you should finish it off and make sure it is not replaced, or your children can't access it, or offer it to friends or neighbours, or donate it to charity.

Wholegrain or Granary breads

Not all brown bread is good for you – it is important to look at the ingredients and make sure there are no added animal fats, hydrogenated oils and sugars such as glucose syrup, molasses or honey. The more unrefined the bread, the lower the GI is likely to be. The following are low-GI breads that I recommend: **soya** and **linseed bread, multigrain/Granary bread, wholegrain, high-fibre bread, rye bread, wholewheat sour dough** and **pumpernickel bread.**

Wholegrain crackers

These are always good as a snack – cover them with the same healthy toppings you would use for toast such as reduced-fat hummus, low-fat cheese spread, peanut butter and reduced-sugar jam. However, some can be very high in fat and many are high GI therefore always check ingredients. Rice crackers and rice cracker snacks are high GI and should be avoided.

Cereals

Cereal with milk makes a great start to the day and can be eaten any time during the day as a quick, easy snack. Beware of cereals targeted at children, as they are generally loaded with sugar and some are also very high in salt. Number one on the list of healthiest cereals is **porridge oats** (traditional large flakes). **Instant oats** are also suitable as long as they do not have unsuitable added ingredients such as extra sugar or added fat. Generally, if the oats are already flavoured (golden syrup flavour for example) then they are unsuitable. Muesli is generally very high in fat and sugars. However if you look around you will find varieties with no added sugar and lower in fat. **All-Bran** is a good low-GI cereal, but can be boring eaten on its own. Try topping it with low-fat yoghurt and chopped fruits, with a sprinkling of nuts or seeds, or blend it into a smoothie for a delicious treat. **Nutri-grain, Just Right, Raisin Bran** and **Sustain** are medium GI and a lot better than many of the other cereals available, such as Rice Krispies, Frosties, Coco Pops and Corn Flakes.

Pasta

Pasta is a popular choice for meals and snacks for children and adults. Pasta can be home-made and prepared by boiling in water or can be quickly heated from a tin. Fortunately most of the popular varieties of pasta are low GI, so you can go wild with different varieties of pasta. **Wholewheat pasta** makes a nice change from white pasta and has a great nutty taste. It is a good source of fibre too. Suitable types include: **linguine, macaroni, spaghetti (dried or canned), vermicelli** and **fettucine.** Avoid creamy sauces as these are high in animal fat (saturated fat). **Spaghetti** or **hoops canned in tomato sauce** are a healthy medium-GI snack but compare brands and choose those with no added sugar and the least salt.

Pasta sauces

Pasta sauces are great to keep in the cupboard and can be used to make a quick healthy pasta dish. But avoid creamy varieties. Always read ingredients and make sure that there is not much added cream, oil or fat (less than 5–10g of fat per 100g) and added sugar (less than 5g per 100g).

Rice

Rice can be a great source of sustained low-GI energy. The best varieties of rice are **brown rice, basmati rice, long grain** and **wild rice.** Make sure you only buy the low and medium GI varieties and avoid the others.

Meat, fish and poultry

Choose lean cuts of beef (**fillet, sirloin** or **topside** are best), lean ham and pork (such as **deli cuts of ham** and **back bacon**), **fully trimmed veal cuts, chicken breasts** (remove the skin), **turkey breasts** (remove the skin), and **all kinds of fish** (include **salmon, fresh tuna, sardines** or **mackerel** at least twice a week).

Dairy

Dairy products are low GI and essential for growing bones. Healthy varieties include: **reduced-fat yellow cheeses** and **sandwich slices, low-fat cottage cheese, low-fat dips** and **sandwich spreads, low-fat yoghurts, semi-skimmed** (low-fat) or **skimmed milk** (fat-free).

Beans, peas and nuts

Beans are very versatile, filling and extremely nutritious. All **beans, peas** and **nuts** are low GI. Nuts are high in healthy types of fat and can be eaten in moderation (a handful) as a filling, healthy snack. **Baked beans** in tomato sauce are great as a snack or served with a meal (choose brands with no added sugar and low salt content). **Soya** can be used as a cheap and healthy meat replacement in casseroles and stews.

Fruit and vegetables – fresh, dried, frozen or canned

Keep a supply of fresh fruit in the kitchen as an easy, healthy snack. **Dried fruit** is a great healthy snack and can be part of a packed lunch. Beware of dried fruit snack bars – many contain added sugar, which raises their GI. **Canned fruit** can be stored in the cupboard and used as a dessert but remember to choose the varieties that contain natural fruit juice rather than syrup or added sugar. Frozen fruit, such as **mixed berries**, is great as a dessert or added to smoothies.

Buy **fresh vegetables** to use in salads and to serve with meals. Try to buy different types of vegetables to make meals more interesting and also to make sure your family is getting the full range of nutrients vegetables provide. **Canned** and **frozen vegetables** can be just as nutritious as fresh (but check the labels for added sugar and salt). Good snack ideas for packed lunches are: **jumbo raisins** (raisin packs for school), **fresh fruit** such as **apples** and **grapes** pre-cut and bagged, and **fruit pieces in natural fruit juice.**

Soups (canned, fresh and instant)

There are many low-fat versions to choose from and many of the normal versions are also low in fat and sugar. Check labels and choose soups that do not contain cream or excessive levels of salt.

Canned vegetarian or meat curries

A convenient pre-prepared meal, canned curries are tasty and easy to prepare. Choose low-GI, low-fat varieties. Add to basmati (or other recommended low-GI rice) and serve with a side salad or vegetables.

Drinks

Water is the best drink. Add **sugar-free cordial** for variety or dilute 200ml of pure fruit juice to make one litre of diluted juice. Choose a **lightly flavoured still** or **sparkling water** that does not contain added sugar. **Diet soft-drinks** can be consumed in moderation (beware excessive amounts can damage teeth). For a sweet, winter-warming treat, try **sugar-free drinking chocolate.**

Condiments

Condiments can be used to flavour foods and spice up the diet and so reduce the amount of salt you need to use. They include vinegars such as balsamic, mustard (not American-style as it contains sugar), chilli sauce, reduced-salt soya sauce, Worcestershire sauce, tomato salsa, spices and herbs. Beware of tomato sauce, as it is high in sugar.

Desserts

Some examples of desserts to keep handy: **custard (low-fat), ice cream (low-fat), light mousses**, and **sugar-free jelly**. Freeze pure fruit juice or diluted sugar-free cordial to make ice-lollies for a treat on hot days.

Chapter 10

Planning meals

It is worthwhile taking the time to plan your family's meals well in advance. This can help to avoid a last-minute rush when you are more likely to make unhealthy food choices.

Breakfast

Breakfast is the most important meal of the day as it helps stabilise blood-sugar levels right from the start, making it less likely the body will crave high-GI foods later on. Many studies have found a relationship between eating breakfast and learning ability, attention span, and general wellbeing. The American Dietetic Association reports that adults who eat breakfast find it easier to lose weight. Children who eat healthy low-GI breakfasts are able to solve problems more effectively, think faster, clearer and are less likely to be irritable. Breakfast is important for all ages, not just children.

Did you know?

In a study of 12 obese teenage boys, those who ate a low-GI breakfast ate significantly less food throughout the rest of the day than those who ate a high-GI breakfast.

Why is it so important that I give my children a filling, healthy breakfast?

Many studies have proven that a healthy breakfast helps children to concentrate better at school and improves behaviour. A healthy low-GI breakfast can ensure that:

- Your children's brains have enough fuel to concentrate until break or lunchtime.
- Hunger and food cravings do not force them to snack on junk food at break time.
- Your children achieve their maximum potential and improve their overall school performance.
- They do not suffer from low-blood-sugar-related mood swings and irritability, which are often the cause of disruptive behaviour in class.
- They walk out of the door feeling full, nourished and healthy.
- They do not overeat at lunchtime and when they get home.
- Their metabolism is fired up for the day. This helps to increase the amount of energy they burn up – which helps prevent unwanted weight gain.

If your children's school provides dinners then they also may offer a breakfast club. Your children could then have breakfast at school before classes start. Alternatively, your children could take food to eat en route to school. Items such as a carton of pure fruit juice or milk, a yoghurt, a piece of fruit, a low-GI sandwich, or a small bag of low-GI dry cereal are ideal.

Breakfast suggestions

- Fruit: All fruit is loaded with fibre and vitamins and is an excellent way to kick-start the day. Try chopping and mixing with a low-fat yoghurt.
- Fruit smoothies: Toss any fruit (such as strawberries, frozen mixed berries) into a blender with plain low-fat yoghurt, fat-free fromage frais or semi-skimmed milk. For a treat, add low-fat ice cream.
- Yoghurt: Buy low-fat natural versions and add reduced-sugar jams or home-made fruit purées to make delicious fruit-flavoured yoghurts.
- Cereals: Oats are best (and taste good with chopped fresh or dried fruit, yoghurt and milk). Make sure that cereals are unrefined and do not have added sugar and fat.
- Bread or toast: Use low-GI breads with one of the following healthy, tasty topping suggestions:
  – Peanut butter – no added sugar.
  – Reduced-sugar jam (add a slice of cheese).
  – Marmite (use a very thin spread as it is high in salt).
  – Banana slices (sprinkled with cinnamon).
  – Cheese slices or low-fat spreads.

– Ham slices.

– Baked beans or canned spaghetti.

Tips

- Always try to include a fruit or vegetable topping on bread and in sandwiches, for example ham and tomato, cheese and tomato, or peanut butter sprinkled with sultanas or chopped dates.
- Serve boiled, scrambled or poached eggs on toast – with tomato (grilled or fresh) and top with fresh parsley. (No real need to use butter or margarine if you're putting something else on toast.)
- Try to eat at least one fruit serving for breakfast. Be creative and combine it with other food, such as smoothies or banana slices on toast.
- Try to avoid high-sugar breakfast cereals and include cooked porridge at least twice a week.

Mid-morning snack

A mid-morning snack is important to keep blood-sugar levels stable and concentration at a peak. Snack suggestions:

- Fruit: Fresh, or tinned in own juice, avoid added sugar or syrup varieties.
- Dried fruit: Try small raisin packs or mixed fruit pieces, no-added-sugar fruit bars.
- Low-fat cheese triangles or cheese slices on wholewheat crackers.

- Yoghurt/ fromage frais: Try the plain versions and sweeten them by blending with fruit or pure fruit purées. For a change, try freezing the yoghurt the night before – it will be nice and slushy by mid-morning!
- Fruit smoothies: Make with fresh fruit and skimmed milk/ yoghurt (freeze for school).
- Wholemeal pitta bread with hummus and ricotta or peanut butter and reduced-sugar jam. It is important to include protein and maximise vegetables and salad ingredients where possible.
- Vegetable fingers: Prepare carrot sticks, celery or cucumber sticks with peanut butter or low-fat cream cheese spread.
- Handful of nuts and raisin mix.
- Check out low-fat dairy desserts as a treat (remember these taste good and are great as once-a-week school treats but do not eat them all the time)!

Lunch

Lunch should be a balanced meal consisting of protein, a starchy food, some dairy foods and some fruit and vegetables. Lunch suggestions:

- Sandwiches – see page 108.
- Canned fish (tuna, salmon, sardines), chicken (such as coronation chicken) on bread or rye crispbreads. Make sure fish is canned in spring water or brine rather than oil.
- Wholemeal pitta pizza – cover with tomato purée, add low-fat cheese and top with different combinations of vegetables, chicken and tuna.

- Wholemeal pasta salad – use leftovers from dinner such as spaghetti bolognaise, pesto pasta – combine with salad and vegetables to create interesting salad mixes.
- A piece of fruit and a yoghurt makes a great ending to a meal.
- A healthy drink (refer to list – page 165).

School dinners and packed lunches

Ever worry what your children are eating at school? There has been a lot of media coverage of school meals and their nutritional inadequacies. At least one meal and one snack per day is eaten at school so teach your children to make healthy meal choices, or follow my guidelines for healthy packed lunches.

Packed lunches

Many children prefer packed lunches to school dinners. A packed lunch can be a good way to ensure your children eat nutritious, healthy food and do not succumb to the high-GI, high-fat choices that are often served up for school lunch. But bear in mind that packed lunches are not stored in a refrigerator so, to prevent any 'nasty' bugs infiltrating your children's food, here are a few ideas to keep packed lunches safe and hygienic:

- Insulation is important to ensure that soup is kept hot in winter and drinks are kept cool in summer. A stainless steel vacuum flask (Thermos) is the best insulator but it is heavier and more expensive than a plastic one.

Healthy school meal choices

CHOOSE:	AVOID:
Baked, grilled chicken or fish dishes	Fish in batter and fried chicken meals
Bean hotpots or baked bean meals	Chips
Tomato based pasta dishes	Cream and cheese pasta dishes
Vegetable or bean soups	Cream of anything soups
Vegetable bakes	Fried or roasted potatoes and cheese toppings
Stews or casseroles	Burgers or hot dogs
Salads and roast vegetables	Chicken nuggets
Fruit and yoghurts	Pizzas

- Invest in an insulated lunch box. Some come equipped with a reusable ice block to keep food cool (store overnight in the freezer). Another idea is to freeze a small carton of pure fruit juice and pack it in the lunchbox to keep the contents cool. It should have thawed by lunchtime, providing a refreshing drink for your children.
- Make sandwiches with frozen, low-GI bread, which will keep the filling cool until it is ready to be eaten. Pack vegetable fillings such as tomato, lettuce and cucumber separately so that the bread does not get soggy.
- Wash vacuum flasks, lunchboxes and any other containers daily with hot water and detergent to keep them clean and safe.

Did you know?

Up to 30 per cent of a child's total food intake is eaten during school time.

- Lunch boxes should contain:

  – Carbohydrate (starchy food), such as bread, rice, pasta with protein source, such as meat, fish, chicken or vegetarian alternative, plus vegetables.

  – Dairy, such as yoghurt, milk drink or cheese.

  – Suitable snack, such as dried fruit or vegetable sticks.

  – Drink of water, milk, sugar-free cordial or fruit juice.

Packed lunch ideas

- Sandwiches: Buy or make them with a low-GI bread and low-fat fillings such as lean chicken breasts, turkey, ham, or tuna, sardines or pilchards. Fill with plenty of salad such as tomatoes, cucumber, lettuce, beetroot, grated carrot, rocket, peppers, onion – any combination is ideal. Use only a thin spread of low-fat margarine or mayonnaise, or for a tasty alternative, try using mustard, pickles, tomato salsa, lemon juice or low-fat salad dressings. Peanut butter is great in sandwiches but use varieties with no added sugar and avoid using butter or margarine (peanut butter contains 50% fat). Adding reduced-sugar strawberry jam or slices of banana makes an interesting and tasty combination.
- Wholemeal wraps make a fun alternative to sandwiches; use your favourite sandwich fillings.

- Combine leftover pasta with low-fat salad dressing or pesto, vegetables, and olives and sprinkle with some parmesan cheese to make a delicious pasta salad.
- Skewer some pieces of cheese, cooked meat and vegetables on wooden skewers and you have simple kebabs.
- A vacuum flask filled with tasty, nutritious soup is ideal on a cold winter's day.
- Add one or two pieces of fruit to the packed lunch.
- Include a suitable drink, such as vegetable juice or 100 per cent pure fruit smoothie, or water in a trendy sports water bottle.

(See www.food.gov.uk for more examples of packed lunch ideas.)

Mid-afternoon snack

It is a good idea to provide another healthy snack mid-afternoon or when children get home from school. This stops the urge to eat junk food. Refer to the mid-morning snack suggestions for ideas and remember that an occasional treat can be included to ensure children do not feel they are missing out, thereby decreasing their desire to eat these treats when you are not around.

Did you know?

One in three children spends his or her pocket money on sweets, chocolates, soft drinks, crisps and snacks on the way to and from school! Encourage your children to spend it on toys, magazines or healthy snacks instead.

Be creative and prepare healthy, tasty treats for children that help satisfy their appetites until dinner is served. Some examples are:

- Low-fat custard drizzled over fruit or reduced-sugar jelly.
- Frozen home-made smoothie desserts on a lolly stick.
- Freeze puréed fruit into ice-tray-size blocks to suck on.

Always have healthy snacks available in the kitchen cupboard – such as wholegrain crackers, dried fruit, unsalted nuts, cheese triangles and low-sugar drinks and sugar-free hot chocolate mixes, so that they can snack on the right types of foods.

Dinner

At the end of a long, busy day, dinner is a time to unwind and spend quality time together as a family.

Dinners should not be excessive. Your body does not need a lot of food before you go to bed as it won't be using much energy while you sleep. The majority of food should be eaten during the day when the food can be used to fuel your daily activities. If you stick to a few main principles when preparing dinner you will be able to prepare wholesome, mouth-watering dinners for the whole family.

Did you know?

A rumbling tummy before bed is a good sign! It means that your stomach is empty and ready to rest while you sleep. Ignore the rumbling for a good night's sleep.

'Light' meals

If you are in a rush and have little time to prepare a meal, choose from a wide variety of healthy or 'light' ranges of ready-prepared meals, available from most supermarkets. Always read the label, making sure the product does not contain excessive added fat, sugar and salt. It should contain a source of protein and a low-GI carbohydrate. If the meal contains little or no vegetables, it is a good idea to quickly prepare extra vegetables or salad on the side.

- Always base the evening meal on low- or medium-GI starchy foods such as pasta or noodles, basmati rice or new potatoes.
- Include different varieties of vegetables and salads.
- Always balance the meal with protein such as lean meats, poultry, eggs, fish, reduced-fat cheese, beans, nuts or pulses.
- Use healthy low-fat cooking methods such as grilling, baking, steaming or boiling and avoid fried foods and batter.

Dinner suggestions

- Soup: Try any home-made stock or tomato based soup (but not cream-based) with vegetables, beans, meat, and pasta such as minestrone. Packet and tin varieties are good too, but beware of salt content. Serve with a wholegrain roll or wholemeal pitta bread.
- Meat: Choose lean meat grilled or barbecued. Avoid fried or fatty meats.

- Fish: Include frozen or fresh fish fillets, grilled or barbecued – they are delicious with salad or vegetables.
- Pasta: Try wholemeal pasta with tomato sauce, bolognaise sauce, macaroni and cheese (use low-fat cheese) or add pre-bought sauces.
- Rice dishes: Brown rice, wholegrain rice, basmati rice and wild rice are really tasty and good for you. You can make great stir-fries with lots of vegetables, served with rice. Make a large quantity and reheat the following night.
- Curries: Some tinned versions are healthy, quick and easy and taste really good. Add to rice and you have an easy and quick meal.
- Burgers: You can make a healthy treat by using lean beef, pork or chicken breast on a wholegrain bun or wholemeal pitta. Load up with lettuce and tomatoes and tomato salsa, mustard and pickles. It is not essential to have chips when you have a burger. However, for a treat and if you have extra time, you can slice new potatoes or sweet potatoes and bake them as a healthy alternative.

Dessert

Some examples of quick and easy dessert treats:

- Frozen mixed berries and low-fat custard.
- Low-fat ice cream with canned fruit (in water or natural fruit juice).
- 'Light' chocolate mousse or dessert treats – check your local supermarket for healthy options that are low in sugar (less than 5g per 100g) and fat (less than 5–10g per 100g).

- Fresh fruit served with low-fat yoghurt.
- Sugar-free jelly with low-fat ice cream.
- Frozen low-fat yoghurt (place tub in freezer a few hours before eating).

Cooking tips

Low-GI, low-fat cooking is very similar to regular cooking but with a few differences:

- Use sugar-free drinking chocolate powder or cocoa powder instead of chocolate in recipes.
- Use evaporated skimmed milk, or half-fat crème fraîche instead of full-fat cream.
- Use only half the amount of oil when sautéeing.
- Create your own light and healthy home-made versions of salad dressings and pasta sauces by reducing the oil content and replacing with vinegar and/or lemon juice.
- Use a non-stick frying pan with a minimal amount of oil to prevent the food sticking to the pan.
- Use a vegetable oil spray to reduce fat in cooking.

Eating out

Eating out can be strewn with potential pitfalls. Birthday parties usually have loads of unhealthy treats on offer such as bowls of crisps, sweets and chocolates, and cakes covered in thick sugary icing. So how do you handle these situations? You would be an ogre not to allow your child to attend the party, yet, you know that they are going to fill up on all the wrong foods – a tricky situation to say the least. Restaurants are another problem area. They are in business to satisfy the taste buds and not to make sure your family eats a healthy diet. Fast food joints are on every corner, leading to the inevitable wail of 'Mum can I have a Happy Meal?' and temper tantrums on the street when you answer 'no'. Why is it that no matter how hard you try at home to provide your family with good nutritious food, you are thwarted the moment you leave your house?

You may be thinking that it is unnecessary to worry about what children eat outside of the home, that it is unfair to spoil their fun. I agree that eating treats is all part of the enjoyment, but if you calculate the number of opportunities children have to indulge their appetites for sugary and fatty treats, you will see that all the birthday parties at school and friends' homes, meals at restaurants, snacks at the cinemas, fast-food meals and holiday eating all add up to a considerable amount of unhealthy food. Eating out twice a week, one movie a week and a birthday party at the weekend is not an unrealistic scenario for many children. It means four occasions in the week when their intake can soar, rendering all your efforts at home worthless in terms of your children's overall health. Rather than restrict your children, it's better to make sure that these situations are well managed allowing you to minimise the risks. In this section, I will explain how to cope on these occasions – without causing embarrassing temper tantrums. Being too strict makes you appear to be a bad parent, but by compromising you can allow your child to enjoy themselves while limiting the damage at the same time.

Birthday parties

Birthday parties are great fun for children and parents. Most parties involve physical activities, which burn lots of energy and help to balance the intake of goodies that children love to eat. However, disaster management is still necessary to reduce excessive amounts of sugar and fat being eaten, which would take days of exercise to get rid of (one chocolate bar takes approximately 3 hours of exercise to burn off!) For older children, it is difficult trying to watch what they eat, but they may suffer intense feelings of guilt if they do not manage to control their intake. Therefore, it is important to teach your children to enjoy themselves – without losing control.

Rules for damage control at birthday parties

- Make sure that you and your children eat a filling low-GI meal before the party so you are not starving hungry by the time you get there. You will then find it easier to make sensible choices and not lose control.
- When you arrive, say your hellos and then take a few minutes with your children to look over all the goodies. Allow them to choose three things that they can eat without feeling guilty. Allow them to enjoy three generous servings of the goodies of their choice. If your children would rather try lots of different things, then allow them to pile up a small plate (side-plate size) of whatever they choose. If they don't want to eat it all at once, keep it with you, allowing them to come over to you for some of the treats at any time they want.

Avoid public criticism

Never humiliate your child by making a scene in public. Children are sensitive and can react badly to criticism in front of their peers. Everyone is allowed to slip up once in a while so it's important not to make them feel bad about it, especially when their friends are around.

- Scout out any low-GI goodies or those that contain fruit and encourage your children to choose those.
- Steer your children in the direction of the physical activities and away from the areas containing food.
- If your children are given a goodie bag – ask them not to open it until you get home and can sort through it, allowing them to choose three items for you to give them at appropriate times.
- Use the goal-and-reward chart (see page 229) to reward good behaviour and accomplishments.

Eating out in restaurants

Eating in restaurants doesn't have to spell disaster. By choosing sensibly and avoiding certain foods, you will ensure that you and your children eat healthily and still have a good time.

Chinese

Chinese food offers many delicious choices for a family night out and meals are usually moderately priced. The hardest part for most children is working out how to use the chopsticks! Avoid the high-GI sticky rice (Jasmine) which is always offered and ask for noodles instead. But the rest is easy, as most traditional dishes are prepared with plenty of vegetables and filling meat, fish and chicken. But beware of those restaurants that are replacing traditional recipes with Westernised versions, which tend to be high in fat, sugar and salt. The following are good choices:

- Broth-based soups such as wonton and hot and sour soup.
- Stir-fried combinations such as seafood, chicken, tofu, meat, all mixed with vegetables. Ask your waiter for a minimum of oil to be used.
- Steamed noodle dishes – ask for chop suey or chow mein – but avoid the fried noodles.
- Steamed fish and vegetable dishes.
- Foods cooked in black bean sauce, oyster sauce, hot mustard sauce and Sichuan sauce.
- A fortune cookie to end the meal is okay. It has only 30 calories and is not very high in fat and sugar.

Indian

Spicy Indian meals are a sure way to send your taste buds into heaven and offer a wide variety of low-GI foods. Indian meals are full of pulses (lentils, chickpeas and beans), chicken, fish and vegetables, and offer basmati rice, which is better than Jasmine rice. However, traditional Indian chefs use an animal fat, ghee, which is an unhealthy saturated fat, so avoid the high-fat meals. The best dishes to order are:

- Vegetable and lentil soups.

- Wholewheat chapattis.
- Chicken, seafood and vegetable biryanis (basmati rice dishes).
- Raita – a side dish made of cucumber salad and yoghurt.
- Chicken, seafood, vegetable curry dishes – order the ones without coconut milk, which is high in saturated fat.
- Chicken or fish vindaloo – it comes in a spicy tomato-based curry sauce.
- Tandoori chicken or fish dishes – these are baked in a clay oven and are low in fat.
- Kebabs.
- Dahls (lentil dishes).

Italian

The most important rule when eating Italian is to avoid the white bread basket, creamy or cheesy sauces and very oily dishes and, instead go for tomato-based pasta dishes, minestrone soups and salads. The best dishes to order are:

- Healthy minestrone or bean soups.
- Italian salads are usually full of interesting ingredients, but choose mixed salads and avoid the oil-drenched, mozzarella and tomato ones (ask for the dressing on the side or use more of the vinegar; go easy on the olive oil – although it is healthy it is still pure fat).
- Tomato-based pasta sauces (but avoid cream- or cheese-filled ravioli or toppings).
- Boiled, grilled or steamed chicken and fish dishes.
- Seafood pasta dishes and stews.

- Thin-crust pizza bases and pile on the vegetable toppings. (Avoid deep-pan pizza and cheese-filled crusts.)
- Poached fruit desserts and lemon sorbets.

Japanese

Definitely a taste worth acquiring – although expensive, it is the healthiest of the lot. Avoid the Jasmine rice but, occasionally, it is okay to order the Californian rolls. These contain fish (and, sometimes, vegetables) which helps to lower the overall GI and it does not come with heavy sauces. The best choices are:

- Miso soup.
- Sashimi – raw fish (packed full of omega-3 oils).
- Edamame – salted and steamed soyabeans.
- Yakitori – grilled chicken kebabs.
- Teriyaki (barbecued) chicken or fish dishes.
- Vegetable or chicken dishes.
- Udon (wheat) noodles or soba (buckwheat) noodles.

Greek

Greek can be a really heavy affair if you do not watch what you are eating. Watch out for fatty filo-filled pastries, feta cheese, potatoes (especially roasted) and generous servings of olive oil. Better choices include fish or chicken dishes served with yoghurt, lemon and rosemary sauces. My recommended Greek choices:

- Bean and lentil soups, vegetable soups, fish soups.
- Tasty shish kebabs – opt for chicken instead of lamb.
- Plaki – baked fish and chicken dishes (ask the waiter to ensure less oil or butter is used).

- Gyro sandwiches.
- Greek salads – only eat a small amount of the feta cheese, which is high in fat.
- Fruit desserts – marinated fruit or compotes.

Mexican (or Tex-Mex)

Mexican restaurants are trouble hotspots and so are best avoided. The food is usually high in fat and refined starches and low on vegetables. Mexican is always best eaten at home where you are in control of the ingredients. Avoid sour cream, guacamole, fried taco shells, and re-fried bean and rice dishes. Instead, make your own Mexican dishes using: shredded lettuce, tomatoes, low-fat cheese, beans, wheat or corn tortilla and fromage frais. Put it all together and hey presto, healthy Mexican food.

Holidays

Kids tend to be very active on holiday and so they can afford to eat more than usual. Try to avoid buffet breakfasts or, if breakfast is included, go for porridge and lots of fresh fruit and yoghurt. Self-catering is a better option for maintaining your health on holiday. That way you can choose what you eat and avoid too many meals eaten in restaurants. Prepare picnics for the beach and avoid the typical high-fat sugar and salt snacks on offer in most holiday resorts.

Fast food and takeaways

There will be times when fast food and takeaways are the easiest options. However, most fast food is high in refined starches, fat and salt and so should be eaten as an occasional treat only. Many people think fast food is a cheap option but home-made meals are definitely cheaper on average. Remember to act as a good role model for your children by not getting too excited whenever you see a fast food sign. If you decide to eat at a fast-food restaurant or have a takeaway then choose wisely:

McDonald's

McDonald's now has a healthy salad menu, including a variety of salads, apples and desserts. The salads are a good choice provided you avoid the dressing, which can send the calories soaring. Be careful of the desserts and the vegetarian burger – they have just as much sugar and energy as McDonald's normal range of foods. Order the grilled chicken caesar salad, grilled chicken ranch salad (with balsamic dressing), pasta salad with chicken, garden side salad, grilled chicken flatbread (no mayonnaise), Quorn burger (no mayonnaise or cheese), Oatso simple (plain), fruit and yoghurt dessert, fruit bag, mineral water, orange juice, diet coke, or semi-skimmed milk.

Burger King

Burger King has a good selection of low-fat choices. Avoid the garlic parmesan toast, which comes with all the salads. Order the flame-grilled chicken salad (with fat-free dressing), flame-grilled shrimp salad (with fat-free dressing), side garden salad (with fat-free dressing), BK veggie (no mayonnaise), chicken whopper (no mayonnaise), low-fat milk, diet coke, water.

Chinese takeaway

The same rules apply to takeaways as to restaurants. However, it is even more important to stick to stir-fries and avoid deep-fried dishes and the Jasmine rice. Takeaway meals tend to be higher in salt, monosodium glutamate and fat.

KFC

Avoid the deep-fried chicken or remove the skin, which is loaded with heart-damaging fat. Choose rice instead of chips and avoid the coleslaw and potato salad. Order a chicken salad, which is far better for you than the deep-fried battered chicken, and have a side order of corn on the cob (no butter), and diet coke or water.

Kebab shops

Order small portions only and do not get a side order of chips. Ask for extra salad with your kebab meal and choose the chicken kebabs, as they contain less fat than the lamb.

Indian takeaway

Follow the same guidelines as for Indian restaurants. Choose dahl and chicken tandoori dishes. Avoid kormas and Indian-style breads, such as naan, as they are usually soaked in oil.

Pizza

Few pizza takeaways offer anything low-fat and low-GI.

Fish and chips

Fish itself is a great food choice but once the batter has been added and deep-fried, plus the serving of high-GI fried chips, make it a no-no!

Fast food and takeaway tips

- Avoid the high-fat extras – that means no mayonnaise, extra cheese or bacon.
- Dressings – pick the fat-free or low-fat alternatives or use a combination of vinegar and lemon juice.
- Choose chicken, rather than fatty meats, and make sure it is grilled and not covered in batter.
- Ketchup is not a vegetable – don't be tempted to use more than one sachet with your meal, it's full of sugar.
- Never order large portions, unless of healthy foods such as salad.
- If you are thirsty, order semi-skimmed milk, or diet soft drinks or water.
- Always ask for your sauce 'on the side' so that you can control the amounts you add to your food. Many fast-food outlets are very liberal with high-fat, high-sugar sauces.
- Instead of chips, order healthy salads (no coleslaw or potato salad), baked beans, corn on the cob and other healthy side dishes.

Cinema

Part of the pleasure of seeing a film is the snacking associated with it. Unfortunately, most of the snacks served at the movies are a health conscious parent's nightmare and they hurt the pocket too! It is best to avoid buying snacks at the cinema and prepare your own at home. Make your own 'movie treat bags' using the following as a guide:

- Low-fat dairy mousse or other healthy desserts.
- Dried fruit and nuts.
- Low-fat frozen yoghurt – take it out of the freezer 15 minutes before you leave and by the time you get to eat it the yoghurt will be the perfect consistency.
- Sugar-free sweets – ask at chemists and health-food stores.
- Sugar-free or 'diet' drinks or water.
- Peanut butter and banana sandwich.
- Sugar-free chewing gum.

If you have not had time to prepare a 'movie treat bag' or you want to indulge and buy goodies at the cinema, these are the best of the worst:

- Small tubs of ice cream.
- A small packet of wine gums.
- A small packet of sucking sweets.
- Unsweetened popcorn.

Portion sizes

It is still possible to gain excess weight, even when you are choosing all the right foods. Eating too much of even healthy products can be a bad thing. Low-GI eating is not a weight-loss diet so I don't expect you to weigh or measure portion sizes, but it is useful to have an idea in your mind of how much food your children need on average in a day.

All children are different and so have different nutritional requirements, but there are some general guidelines you can follow. If your child is obese and you would like to restrict their intake to promote slow weight loss make sure you do not give them less than the recommended amounts of food per day. They need at least this amount to grow properly and obtain all the necessary vitamins and minerals their body requires.

Carbohydrates (starchy foods):

Four to six portions per day

These portions of low-GI carbohydrates should be spread throughout the day and eaten with every meal, including snacks. One portion is:

- One slice of low-GI bread (such as Granary).
- Six tablespoons of low-GI breakfast cereal or porridge.
- Four wholewheat crisp breads.
- One wholemeal roll.
- Six tablespoons of macaroni, brown rice, basmati or barley.
- Two small new potatoes.
- Two tablespoons of wholegrain flour.
- ¼ cup cooked yam, sweet potato or squash.

Fruit and vegetables:

Five portions per day

It is important to eat a wide variety of fruit and vegetables so that you get the complete range of all the important nutrients they provide. One portion of fruit and vegetables is:

- One whole medium-sized fruit such as a pear, apple or orange.
- A couple of small fruits (such as plums) or a cupful of very small fruits (such as grapes or berries).
- Half to one tablespoon of dried fruits (such as raisins, prunes or apricots).
- One piece of a big fruit (such as half a grapefruit, a wedge of melon, a couple of rings of pineapple, or half an avocado).
- Two tablespoons of raw, cooked, frozen or canned vegetables.
- A bowl of salad.
- A glass of fruit juice (200ml).

Remember:

- No more than one glass (200ml) of pure fruit juice a day (fruit juice counts as one portion only – no matter how many you have).
- Potatoes are classified as a starchy food and not a vegetable.
- Although five sounds like a lot, portion sizes are small.
- Fruit is an excellent substitute for sugary foods.
- Try to be creative and combine fruit with dairy foods or in cereals, or on toast.

Meat and meat alternatives:

Two to three portions per day

These foods include meat, fish, chicken, turkey, ham, beans, pulses, lentils, eggs and vegetarian alternatives – Quorn and soya products. They are very important for growing bodies as they provide the building blocks for the body and meats are a good source of iron. One portion of meat is:

- Two slices of cold ham, turkey or chicken.
- One medium chicken breast or two drumsticks.
- Three thin slices of roast beef.
- Two serving spoonfuls of beef stew.
- Around 140g steak or beef rump steak grilled.
- One veal escalope.
- Two serving spoonfuls of beef mince.
- Two beef sausages.
- Three grilled lean bacon rashers.
- One frozen grilled beefburger.

Remember:

- Choose lean cuts of meat.
- White meat is always lower in fat than the darker meat (for example, chicken breasts are better than chicken thighs).
- The skin contains most of the fat – a simple way to reduce saturated fat is to remove it before cooking.

One portion of fish is:

- One fillet of steamed/grilled/baked cod, haddock, sole, plaice.
- One tuna, salmon or trout steak.

Top tip

An easy way to remember protein portion sizes is to measure it against the palm your hand. A portion of meat or fish is roughly one third of the size of the palm of your hand (applies to adults and children of all ages).

- One small can of tuna, salmon, mackerel, sardines (canned in spring water or brine).
- Four grilled cod fish fingers – (in breadcrumbs not in batter).
- Two fillets of baked kippers or grilled herring.

Remember:

- Eat oily fish at least twice a week (see page 79). Fresh tuna counts as an oily fish but canned tuna does not. See www.food.gov.uk for a list of oily fish.
- Always choose fish canned in spring water or brine, rather than vegetable oil.

One portion of vegetarian protein is:

- One teacupful of cooked lentils or beans.
- Half a large can of chilli beans, chickpeas, or lentils.
- One small can of baked beans in tomato sauce (reduced sugar and salt).
- A 100g portion of Tofu or Quorn.

One portion of egg is:

- One boiled, scrambled or poached egg.

Top tip

If your children do not eat the recommended serving of one portion of oily fish per week then buy eggs containing omega-3 as an alternative source.

Dairy products:

Three low-fat servings per day

Three servings per day is enough to provide all the calcium your children need. As it contains a high amount of saturated fats, you need to choose low-fat or fat-free types. One portion is:

- One glass (200ml) of low-fat or skimmed (fat-free) milk.
- One low-fat yoghurt (150g tub).
- One fat-free tub of fromage frais (200g).
- One matchbox size piece of cheese (30g) or two triangles.
- Half a tin (200g) of low-fat custard.

Did you know?

White cheese is naturally lower in fat than yellow cheese. Softer cheeses contain less fat than hard cheese (for example, cottage cheese is lower in fat than Cheddar or Edam).

Chapter 11

Low-GI recipes for the whole family

All the recipes contained in this book are produced using low-GI ingredients and are also low in unhealthy fats. We have tried to keep the recipes simple and easy to prepare and would encourage you to make them with your children. Children are far more likely to try new foods when they have played a part in their preparation. Assign them tasks that you feel they can carry out safely and remember to keep a close eye on them at all times. Beware of hot liquids and surfaces, and sharp knives. Some people have the perception that healthy eating is expensive, so to dispel this illusion, we have costed the recipes (2005 prices) in order to illustrate just how cheap it is to eat nutritious, filling, low-GI foods. The preparation and cooking times have also been included to help you manage your time effectively.

Breakfast

Fruity Porridge

SERVES 4

Total Cost: 47p (12p per portion)

Preparation Time: 2 minutes

Cooking Time: 8 minutes

100g	Porridge oats
75g	Dried mixed fruit/dried sultanas/dried raisins
600ml	Skimmed milk

Place the porridge oats, the dried fruit and milk in a glass bowl suitable for the microwave.

Stir well and cook in a 650w microwave for 4 minutes (reduce cooking time if the wattage on the microwave is higher and increase if lower).

Stir and cook for a further 3 minutes.

Alternatively, place the oats, fruit and milk in a medium-sized saucepan and cook over a moderate heat for 7–8 minutes, stirring until thick and creamy.

Chef's Note:

- Add more milk if it starts to become too thick.

Breakfast Special

SERVES 4

Total Cost: £1.78p (45p per portion)

Preparation Time: 5 minutes

Cooking Time: 3 minutes

75g	Rice flakes
500ml	Skimmed milk
150g	Grated apple (unpeeled)
1 tbsp	Clear honey or 2 tbsp granulated sweetener
50g	Nuts (hazelnuts, pecans, walnuts, almonds)
25g	Pumpkin seeds
25g	Sunflower seeds

Place the rice flakes in a medium-sized non-stick saucepan and stir in the milk. Add the grated apple into the rice mixture and cook over a moderate heat for 3 minutes.

Remove from the heat and stir in the honey or sweetener, nuts and seeds.

Serve on its own or topped with fresh fruit

Chef's Note:

- Soya or semi-skimmed milk may be used as an alternative to skimmed milk.
- More milk can be added to give a thinner consistency.

Oaty Pancakes

MAKES 8

Total Cost: £1.25p (16p each)

Preparation Time: 5 minutes

Cooking Time: 15 minutes

Pancakes:

25g	Medium oatmeal
100g	Wholemeal self-raising flour
1 tsp	Baking powder
1	Large egg
150ml	Skimmed milk/soya milk
1 tbsp	Granulated sweetener or 1 tbsp clear honey
1 tsp	Vanilla essence
1 tbsp	Mild olive oil or vegetable oil

Apricot Compôte:

125g	Ready-to-eat dried apricots
250ml	Water

Alternative Topping:

4 tsp	Peanut butter (no added salt or sugar)
2	Bananas, sliced

Place all the pancake ingredients except the oil, in a medium-sized bowl and whisk for 1 minute with an electric mixer. Cover and leave to stand while making the apricot compôte.

Place the apricots and water in a small saucepan and cook over a gentle heat for 5–7 minutes (taking care not to allow the liquid to evaporate).

Pour into a food processor or blender and process until smooth. Transfer to a small dish.

To make the pancakes – heat the oil in a medium-sized non-stick frying pan. Once the oil is hot, pour the excess oil into a small heatproof dish.

Drop tablespoonfuls of batter into the base of the frying pan to produce 3–4 pancakes, cooking at the same time. Do not allow them to touch.

When bubbles appear, turn the pancakes over and cook for a further minute or so until golden brown. Remove the pancakes from the pan and allow to cool on a wire rack.

Repeat the process until all the batter is used.

Top with the apricot compôte or spread thinly with peanut butter and top with slices of banana.

Chef's Note:

- This recipe calls for oatmeal, not porridge oats. Oatmeal is available from most supermarkets and health-food stores.
- Try other ready-to-eat dried fruits as an alternative to apricots.
- Low-fat natural yoghurt also makes a delicious topping for the pancakes.

Eggy Bread with Bacon and Tomato

SERVES 2

Total Cost: £1.07p (54p per portion)

Preparation Time: 2 minutes

Cooking Time: 5–7 minutes

3	Rashers of back bacon, fat cut off and discarded
2	Large tomatoes cut into thick slices
1	Large egg
125ml	Skimmed milk
	Sprinkle of black/white pepper
2 slices	Multigrain or seeded bread

Heat a non-stick frying pan and cook the rashers of bacon. Add the slices of tomato and cook until just beginning to soften. Remove from the pan and keep warm.

Meanwhile, break the egg into a shallow dish and mix with the milk.

Lay the bread into the egg and milk mixture, turn over and then lay carefully into the hot frying pan.

Cook for approximately 1 minute then turn over and cook the other side.

Serve the eggy bread topped with the bacon and tomato.

Chef's Note:

- The back bacon used for this dish can be smoked or unsmoked. If using smoked back bacon, no further salt needs to be added, just sprinkle with pepper.

Lunch

Winter Vegetable Soup

SERVES 6

Total Cost: £2.04p (34p per portion)

Preparation Time: 15 minutes

Cooking Time: 35 minutes

1 tbsp	Vegetable oil or mild olive oil
1	Large onion, peeled and sliced
1	Red pepper, deseeded and thickly sliced
1	Clove garlic, peeled and crushed
200g	Swede, peeled and sliced
1 medium	Parsnip, peeled and sliced
2 sticks	Celery, sliced
500ml	Vegetable stock (made up of 1 vegetable stock cube and boiling water)
250ml	Skimmed milk (use only what is required)
1 tbsp	Parsley, finely chopped

Heat the oil in a large saucepan and cook the onion and red pepper until softened but not coloured. This takes about 5 minutes.

Add the garlic and cook for a further 30 seconds. Add the swede, parsnip, celery and stock and cook over a medium heat for 25–30 minutes.

Place the soup in a liquidiser or blender and process until smooth.

Pour into a clean saucepan, add sufficient milk to give a pouring consistency and heat through.

Serve sprinkled with parsley.

Curried Tuna in Pitta Bread

SERVES 4

Total Cost: £2.79p (70p per portion)

Preparation Time: 10 minutes

Cooking Time: Nil

200g	Can tuna steak in spring water
75g	Cucumber, cut into small pieces
1 large	Tomato, quartered, deseeded and cut into small cubes
2	Spring onions, topped, tailed and finely chopped
1–2 tsp	Curry paste (optional)
3 heaped tbsp	Low-fat fromage frais
4	Wholemeal pittas or pitta pockets
8	Lettuce leaves, torn
	Salt and pepper to taste

In a medium-sized bowl, mix the tuna with the cucumber, tomato, spring onion, curry paste (if using) and fromage frais.

Open up the pitta bread/pockets and place a few pieces of torn lettuce inside each one, then top up with the curried tuna mixture.

Serve immediately.

Chef's Note:

- The strength of the curry paste will depend on your personal choice.
- As an alternative to curry paste, use either the zest of one orange or zest of one lemon or 1 tbsp finely chopped fresh mint.
- If you do not want to serve the pittas immediately, keep the tuna mixture in a bowl in the fridge and fill the pitta bread/pockets just before serving.

Vegetable Fritters

MAKES 6 (SERVES 2)

Total Cost: £1.70p (85p per portion)

[cost only includes one dip]

Preparation Time: 10 minutes

Cooking Time: 6 minutes for each batch

Fritters:

1	Red onion, peeled and finely sliced
100g	Fine green beans, trimmed and finely sliced
10g	Parsley/coriander, roughly chopped
1	Medium-sized egg
2	Large tomatoes cut into quarters. Discard seeds and cut into 1cm cubes
40g	Plain wholemeal flour
	Salt and pepper to taste
1 tbsp	Mild olive oil

Dips:

4 tbsp	Low-fat natural yoghurt
¼ –½ tsp	Chinese five spice
OR	
4 tbsp	Low-fat natural yoghurt
100g	Cucumber, finely chopped
½ tsp	Mint sauce

In a medium-sized bowl, mix together the onion, beans, parsley/coriander, egg, tomato, flour and seasoning.

Heat the oil in a medium-sized frying pan and place a large tablespoon of mixture into the pan, adding 2–3 further spoons of mixture (depending on size of pan), spacing them well apart.

Cook for 2–3 minutes on each side until golden brown.

To make either dip, combine the listed ingredients together. Serve the hot fritters with your choice of dips.

Lentil Purée with Toasted Pitta

SERVES 2–4

Total Cost: £1.48 (37p per portion)

Preparation Time: 10 minutes

Cooking Time: 20 minutes

150g	Red lentils
800ml	Cold water
2 tbsp	Vegetable or mild olive oil
1	Large onion, finely chopped

2	Cloves garlic, peeled and finely chopped
1 tsp	Ground coriander
½ tsp	Ground cumin
100ml	Vegetable stock (made up of 1 vegetable stock cube and boiling water)
150ml	Cold water
2–3	Wholemeal pitta breads

Rinse the lentils and place in a medium-sized saucepan. Add the cold water and bring to the boil. Reduce the heat and simmer for 10 minutes, scooping off and discarding the froth with a slotted spoon.

Place the lentils in a sieve to drain, discarding the liquid. Put the lentils to one side.

Heat the oil in a clean medium-sized saucepan and cook the onion over a low heat for 3–5 minutes stirring occasionally until softened but not browned.

Add the garlic, ground coriander and cumin and cook for a further minute. Stir in the lentils and add the stock and cold water, then cook over a moderate heat for 10 minutes, stirring occasionally until most of the liquid has been absorbed. The consistency should be sloppy.

Preheat the grill to a moderate heat. Place the pitta breads under the grill and toast lightly. Then cut into 5cm strips.

Serve the spicy lentils with the strips of pitta bread.

Dinner

Chicken Curry

SERVES 4

Total Cost: £7.33p (£1.83p per portion)

Preparation Time: 15 minutes

Cooking Time: 15 minutes

4 sprays	Olive oil spray or 1 tbsp mild olive oil
1	Onion, peeled and finely chopped
125g	Carrots, peeled and cut into 5cm sticks
2	Cloves garlic, peeled and crushed
4	Skinless, boneless chicken breasts, cut into thin strips
1	Red pepper, deseeded and thickly sliced
125g	Broccoli florets, cut each large floret into four pieces
1	Large courgette, topped, tailed and thickly sliced
500g	Jar low-fat curry sauce
200g	Basmati rice
6	Cherry tomatoes
20g	Fresh coriander, roughly chopped
150ml	Low-fat natural yoghurt (optional)

Heat the oil in a large non-stick saucepan and cook the onion and carrot over a gentle heat for approximately 3–4 minutes. Add the garlic and cook for a further minute, stirring occasionally.

Add the chicken strips and cook, stirring continually until sealed on all sides.

Add the pepper, broccoli and courgette then stir in the curry sauce. Cover with a lid and cook over a moderate heat for 10–14 minutes, stirring occasionally.

While the curry is cooking, cook the rice according to the packet instructions.

Add the tomatoes to the curry for the last 5 minutes of the cooking time.

Serve the rice with the curry and sprinkle with coriander. Serve with a spoonful of cooling yoghurt (optional).

Chef's Note:

- Choose a curry sauce that is less than 5g fat and less than 5g of sugar per 100g. The curry sauce used is from Sainsbury's 'Be Good to Yourself' range.

Turkey Burgers with Tomato Salsa

SERVES 4 (MAKES 8 BURGERS)

Total Cost: £3.33p (42p per burger)

Preparation Time: 10–15 minutes

Cooking Time: 6 minutes for each batch

For the Burgers:

1	Onion, peeled and very finely chopped
1–2	Cloves garlic, peeled and crushed (optional)
100g	Carrots, peeled and grated
500g	Lean turkey mince (less than 6 per cent fat) or lean minced beef (less than 10 per cent fat)

2 tbsp	Tomato purée
10g	Fresh coriander/parsley, finely chopped
	Salt and pepper
25g	Wholemeal plain flour
1 tbsp	Mild olive oil or vegetable oil

For the Salsa:

2	Medium-sized tomatoes, quartered, deseeded and cut into 1cm cubes
4	Spring onions, finely chopped
1	Green chilli, deseeded and finely chopped (optional)
10g	Coriander/parsley, finely chopped
Juice	½ lemon

To make the burgers – place the onion, garlic, carrots, mince, tomato purée and herbs in a large bowl and mix together. Alternatively, place these ingredients in a food processor and process briefly until well combined. Season with a little salt and pepper.

Shape the mixture into 8 x 8cm rounds, 2cm deep. Coat each burger lightly in the wholemeal flour.

Heat the oil in a medium-sized non-stick frying pan and cook the burgers four at a time over a medium heat for approximately 3 minutes per side until golden brown and hot all the way through, with no pink juices remaining.

To make the salsa – combine all the ingredients in a small bowl and cover. Leave to stand while cooking the burgers to allow the flavours to develop.

Serve the burgers with the salsa and a watercress, spinach and rocket salad.

Chef's Note:

- To give the 'true' burger effect, try toasting slices of multi-grain bread and cutting out circles using a teacup or ramekin dish, approximately the same size as the burgers. Sandwich the burgers and salsa in between.

Moroccan-style Tagine

SERVES 4

Total Cost: £3.99p (£1.00p per portion)

Preparation Time: 20 minutes

Cooking Time: 30 minutes

1 tbsp	Mild olive oil
1	Large onion, peeled and cut into thick slices
1-2	Cloves garlic, peeled and chopped
1 tsp	Ground coriander
1 tsp	Ground cumin
5cm	Piece of fresh root ginger, peeled and grated
400g	Can chopped tomatoes
175g	Carrots, peeled and sliced
500ml	Vegetable stock (made up of 1 vegetable stock cube and boiling water)
1	Cinnamon stick, broken in half
1	Courgette, topped, tailed and thickly sliced

250g	Cauliflower florets cut into smaller pieces if too large
410g	Can chickpeas, drained
250g	Couscous
20g	Fresh coriander, roughly chopped

To Serve:

4 tbsp	Low-fat natural yoghurt

Heat the oil in a non-stick saucepan and cook the onion over a low heat until softened but not coloured. This takes approximately 3–4 minutes.

Add the garlic, coriander, cumin and ginger and cook for a further minute.

Stir in the tomatoes, carrots, stock and cinnamon stick and cook over a medium heat for 10 minutes.

Add the courgette and cauliflower and cover with a lid. Cook for 10 minutes. Add the chickpeas and cook for a further 5 minutes.

Meanwhile cook the couscous according to the packet instructions.

Remove and discard the cinnamon stick.

Serve the couscous with the vegetable tagine and top with a spoonful of yoghurt.

Chef's Note:

- This dish can be made using alternative vegetables, such as green beans, broccoli or baby corn.

Salmon Fishcakes with Lemon Sauce

MAKES 6 FISHCAKES

Total Cost: £6.72p (£1.12 per fishcake)

Preparation Time: 10 minutes

Cooking Time: 20 minutes

For the Fishcakes:

300g	Salmon fillets
450g	Sweet potato, peeled and thickly sliced
Zest	1 lemon
4	Spring onions, finely chopped
20g	Coriander/parsley, finely chopped
25g	Wholemeal plain flour
4 sprays	Olive oil spray or 1 tbsp mild olive oil

For the Sauce:

Juice	1 lemon
1 tbsp	Arrowroot
2 tbsp	Granulated sweetener

Place the salmon fillets in a shallow saucepan or frying pan and pour in enough water to just cover the fish. Cook over a gentle heat until the fish turns opaque and begins to flake.

Remove the fish from the pan, take off the skin, flake and put to one side. Reserve 150ml of the stock the fish was cooked in (add extra water if necessary to make up the quantity).

Meanwhile, cook the sweet potatoes in boiling water until soft. Drain and mash. Allow to cool.

Mix the salmon with the sweet potatoes, lemon zest, spring onions and coriander/parsley. Shape into six even-sized patties about 7cm in diameter and 2cm deep.

Lightly coat in wholemeal flour.

Heat the frying pan, add oil and cook the fishcakes for approximately 3 minutes on each side until golden brown and hot right through. Keep warm.

To make the sauce – blend the lemon juice, arrowroot, stock and sweetener together in a small saucepan and bring to the boil, stirring continuously.

Serve the fishcakes with the lemon sauce and a selection of fresh vegetables or a salad.

Chef's Note:

- The artificial sweetener used in this recipe is Canderel.

Spaghetti-style Bolognaise

SERVES 4

Total Cost: £2.85p (71p per portion)

Preparation Time: 10 minutes

Cooking Time: 25 minutes

2 sprays	Olive oil spray or 1 tbsp vegetable or mild olive oil
1	Onion, peeled and chopped
1	Clove garlic, peeled and crushed

500g	Lean turkey mince (less than 6 per cent fat) or lean minced beef (less than 10 per cent fat)
150g	Carrots, peeled and grated
400g	Can chopped tomatoes
2 tbsp	Tomato purée
420g	Can mixed bean salad
2 tsp	English mustard powder
½ tsp	Tabasco® sauce
200g	Spaghetti pasta

Give two sprays of olive oil or add one tablespoon of oil to a medium-sized non-stick saucepan. Add the onion and cook over a low heat for 3–4 minutes, stirring occasionally until the onion is softened, but not coloured.

Add the garlic and cook for a further 30 seconds.

Stir in the turkey mince and cook, stirring regularly until the meat is light in colour all over.

Add the carrots, chopped tomatoes, tomato purée, mixed beans, mustard powder and Tabasco® sauce. Stir well, then cover with a lid and reduce the heat. Cook for 15 minutes.

Cook the spaghetti in boiling water according to the packet instructions and then drain.

Serve with the bolognaise sauce.

Chef's Note:

- Any leftover bolognaise mixture can be frozen for another occasion.

Smoked Tomato Sauce

SERVES 4

Total Cost: £1.86p (47p per portion)

Preparation Time: 5 minutes

Cooking Time: 10 minutes

1	Rasher of smoked back bacon
1	Red pepper, deseeded and finely chopped
1	Onion, peeled and finely chopped
2	Cloves garlic, peeled and crushed
2 tbsp	Fresh thyme leaves
400g	Can chopped tomatoes

Cook the bacon in a medium-sized non-stick saucepan until golden.

Add the pepper and onion and cook for a further minute. Add the garlic, thyme and canned tomatoes and cook over a moderate heat for 5–7 minutes.

Pour into a food processor or blender and process until smooth.

To make it extra smooth, press the sauce through a sieve.

Return the sauce to a clean saucepan, season to taste then heat through.

Serve over Spicy Chicken Kebabs (see opposite).

Chef's Note:

- This sauce is also delicious served over hot cooked pasta or with grilled chicken, microwaved fish or vegetarian sausages.

Spicy Chicken Kebabs

SERVES 4

Total Cost: £3.53p (88p per portion)

500g	Chicken mince
10g	Fresh parsley, finely chopped
1	Onion, peeled and very finely chopped
2 tbsp	Balti curry paste
1–2	Cloves garlic, peeled and finely chopped (optional)
	Salt and black pepper to taste

Preheat the oven to 190°C/375°F/Gas Mark 5.

Place the chicken mince in a food processor with the parsley, onion, garlic and curry paste. Process together and then add the seasoning. Alternatively, place the ingredients in a bowl and mix well together.

Shape into 16 balls and thread onto 4 metal or wooden skewers and lay on a non-stick baking tray.

Cook in the oven for 15 minutes.

Serve with Smoked Tomato Sauce (see opposite) and a green salad.

Chef's Note:

- If using wooden skewers, soak in cold water for 1 hour before threading food onto them.
- These kebabs can also be grilled on a barbecue.
- Turkey mince can be used as an alternative to chicken mince.

Vegetarian Sausages

MAKES 8

Total Cost: £1.27p (16p per sausage)

Preparation Time: 10 minutes

Cooking Time: 5–7 minutes

50g	Fresh breadcrumbs from wholegrain bread
50g	Medium/fine oatmeal
4 tbsp	Low-fat fromage frais
1 tbsp	Fresh parsley, finely chopped
1 tbsp	Fresh thyme leaves
1 tsp	English mustard powder
¼ tsp	Salt
1	Onion, peeled and very finely chopped
1	Egg, separated, egg white placed on a flat plate
25g	Plain wholemeal flour
2 tbsp	Vegetable oil or mild olive oil

In a large bowl, mix together all the ingredients except for the egg white and wholemeal flour.

Divide into 8 portions and roll each into a sausage shape.

Roll the sausage shapes in the egg white and then into the flour.

Heat the oil in a medium/large non-stick frying pan and cook the vegetarian sausages, turning frequently until golden brown on all sides and hot all the way through, approximately 5–7 minutes.

Chef's Note:

- Serve the sausages with Smoked Tomato Sauce (see page 150) or Red Pepper Sauce (see below) and a green salad.

Red Pepper Sauce

SERVES 4

Total Cost: £1.98p (50p per portion)

Preparation Time: 2 minutes

Cooking Time: 15 minutes

1 tsp	Vegetable oil or mild olive oil
1	Onion, peeled and finely chopped
2	Cloves garlic, peeled and crushed
2	Red peppers, char-grilled (see Chef's Note) and cut into strips
1	Vegetable stock cube
125ml	Boiling water

Heat the oil in a small saucepan and cook the onion over a moderate heat for approximately 4 minutes, stirring occasionally until softened but not coloured.

Add the garlic and cook for a further 30 seconds.

Add the peppers, stock cube and water and cook over a gentle heat for approximately 7–10 minutes.

Pass through a sieve. If the sauce is too thick, thin down with a little boiling water.

Chef's Note:

- To char-grill peppers – preheat the oven to 220°C/425°F/Gas Mark 7. Place the peppers on a non-stick roasting tray and brush lightly with oil. Cook until the skin is black, turning regularly. Remove from the oven and wrap immediately in cling film until cold. Peel off and discard the skin and the seeds. Cut the flesh into strips.
- This sauce can be served over pasta, chicken or fish. It is also delicious with vegetarian sausages.

Moussaka

SERVES 6

Total Cost: £4.63p (77p per portion)

Preparation Time: 10–15 minutes

Cooking Time: 35 minutes

2 tbsp	Mild olive oil or vegetable oil
1	Large aubergine, topped and sliced
1	Onion, peeled and finely chopped
500g	Lean turkey mince or chicken mince (less than 6 per cent fat) or lean minced beef (less than 10 per cent fat)
1 tbsp	Ground coriander
1 tsp	Ground cinnamon
400g	Can chopped tomatoes
200ml	Low-fat Greek-style natural yoghurt
2	Large eggs

Preheat the oven to 180°C/350°F/Gas Mark 4.

Heat 1 tablespoon of oil in a large non-stick frying pan and cook the aubergine slices on both sides. Then remove from the pan and drain on absorbent kitchen paper.

Add the other tablespoon of oil and heat and then add the onion and cook over a moderate heat until softened but not browned.

Place the mince in the pan and continue to cook until browned, approximately 3–4 minutes.

Stir in the coriander and cinnamon and cook for a further minute, then add the chopped tomatoes.

Transfer to a 28 x 17cm ovenproof dish.

Lay the aubergine slices over the meat.

Mix the yoghurt and eggs together and pour over the top.

Cook in the oven for 25–30 minutes until the top is golden brown.

Chef's Note:

- Greek-style yoghurt is used in this recipe because it is slightly higher in fat and less lightly to 'split' under the intense heat of the oven.

Dessert

Mango Fool

SERVES 6

Total Cost: £2.90p (48p per portion)

Preparation Time: 5 minutes

Cooking Time: Nil

1	Ripe mango, stoned and peeled
425g	Carton low-fat custard (less than 2 per cent fat)
450ml	Carton Greek-style low-fat natural yoghurt (less than 3 per cent fat)
	Mint leaves (optional)

Remove the flesh from the mango, reserving a few pieces for decoration, and place the remainder in a food processor.

Process until smooth.

Layer the custard, yoghurt and mango in tall glasses or a glass bowl, finishing with a layer of yoghurt. Chill for at least 2 hours before serving.

Decorate with the reserved pieces of mango and mint leaves.

Chef's Note:

- This dessert does not freeze well.

Plum Crumble

SERVES 4

Total Cost: £2.14p (54p per portion)

Preparation Time: 5 minutes

Cooking Time: 30 minutes

500g	Plums, quartered and stoned
2–3 tbsp	Artificial sweetener or 2 tbsp honey
50g	Wholemeal plain flour
25g	Reduced-fat spread
25g	Porridge oats

Preheat the oven to 180°C/350°F/Gas Mark 4.

Place the plums in a shallow ovenproof dish and sprinkle with 1–2 tablespoons of granulated sweetener; alternatively drizzle with 2 tablespoons of clear honey.

Pour the flour into a small bowl and rub in the fat until it resembles breadcrumbs.

Stir in the porridge oats and a further tablespoon of sweetener.

Sprinkle the crumble mixture over the plums and cook in the oven for 30 minutes.

Chef's Note:

- The artificial sweetener used in this recipe is Canderel.
- Apples, apricots or peaches can be used instead of plums.

Choccy Rice Pudding

SERVES 2–4

Total Cost: 42p (11p per portion)

Preparation Time: 2 minutes

Cooking Time: 20 minutes

50g	Basmati rice
6 level tsp	Instant low-calorie hot chocolate drink powder (contains artificial sweetener)
500ml	Boiling water

Place the rice in a medium-sized non-stick saucepan and add the chocolate drink powder and the boiling water.

Cook over a medium/low heat for approximately 20 minutes, stirring occasionally. Take care not to have the heat too high or the liquid will evaporate. The rice should be 'just' cooked, surrounded by creamy chocolate liquid.

This dessert can be eaten hot or cold. It is delicious cold, topped with fresh raspberries and a spoonful of yoghurt.

Chef's Note:

- Any of the different flavours of Highlights or similar low-calorie hot chocolate powder can be used.

Raspberry Fluff

SERVES 6–8

Total Cost: £4.05 (51p per portion)

Preparation Time: 10–15 minutes to allow for jelly to cool

Cooking Time: Nil

26g	Pack of raspberry flavour jelly, sugar-free
125ml	Boiling water
125ml	Cold water
410g	Can light evaporated milk, chilled
150g	Raspberries

Empty both sachets of jelly crystals into a measuring jug and pour over the boiling water, stirring until the crystals have dissolved, then stir in the cold water.

Allow the jelly to cool but not set.

Using an electric mixer, whisk the milk until thick and fluffy (this takes approximately 2 minutes) and then whisk in the cooled jelly.

Pour into a large bowl or 6–8 small dishes. Cover and chill for a few hours to set.

Decorate with fresh raspberries.

Chef's Note:

- Chill the evaporated milk in the fridge for as long as possible before use.
- Any flavour of jelly can be used.
- Any fresh fruit can be served with this dessert.

Snacks

Orange and Blueberry Muffins

MAKES 12

Total Cost: £3.89p (32p per muffin)

Preparation Time: 10 minutes

Cooking Time: 15 minutes

300g	Cooking apples, peeled and grated
Zest and juice	2 oranges
2 tbsp	Mild olive oil
8 level tbsp	Granulated sweetener
250g	Wholemeal self-raising flour
1 tsp	Baking powder
1	Sachet pasteurised egg white or 2 egg whites
100g	Fresh blueberries
12	Paper muffin cases

Preheat the oven to 180°C/350°F/Gas Mark 4.

Place the grated apple, orange zest and juice, oil and sweetener into a large bowl and mix together.

Using a metal spoon, carefully fold in the flour and baking powder.

Make up the pasteurised egg white powder according to the manufacturer's instructions, or whisk the two egg whites until they form soft peaks.

Fold the egg whites and blueberries into the apple mixture.

Place a tablespoon of the mixture into each of the muffin cases.

Bake in the oven for 12–15 minutes until well risen and 'springy' on the top when lightly pressed. Remove from the oven and cool on a wire rack.

When cooled, store in an airtight container in the fridge. Use within 3–4 days.

Chef's Note:

- If using fairy cake cases, the cooking time should be reduced. Also more fairy cakes will be made from the mixture.
- The artificial sweetener used in this recipe is Splenda.
- Ideal for lunch boxes.

Fruity Tea Bread

MAKES 10–12 SLICES

Total Cost: £1.48p (12p per slice)

Preparation Time: 20 minutes (this includes soaking time for fruit)

Cooking Time: 40 minutes

175g	Dried fruit/raisins/sultanas
300ml	Strong tea; 2 teabags
20g	Granulated sweetener
6	Cardamom pods (optional), crush seeds and discard pods
Zest and juice	1 orange
1 large	Egg

300g	Wholemeal self-raising flour
1 tsp	Baking powder
1 tsp	Ground cinnamon

Line a 1kg (22 x 12 x 7cm) loaf tin with baking parchment or cut a piece of parchment large enough to cover the base of the tin and lightly oil the sides.

Place the dried fruit in a medium-sized heatproof bowl and pour over the tea.

Stir in the sweetener and cardamom seeds (if used). Loosely cover and leave to stand overnight or until the tea is cold, approximately 20 minutes.

Preheat the oven to 160°C/325°F/Gas Mark 3.

Stir the orange zest, juice, egg, flour, baking powder and cinnamon into the fruit mixture and pour into the tin. Smooth the surface with a wet knife.

Bake in the oven for 35–40 minutes. To test if it is cooked, insert a skewer and if it comes out clean, it is cooked.

Remove from the oven and leave in the tin to cool for 10 minutes before turning out onto a wire rack to cool completely. Keep refrigerated.

Chef's Note:

- The artificial sweetener used in this recipe is Splenda.
- This fruity tea bread freezes well.
- Ideal for lunch boxes.

Spiced Nuts

(No whole nuts for under fives or those with a nut allergy.)

Total Cost: £1.07p

Preparation Time: 1 minute

Cooking Time: 3 minutes

100g	Mixed nuts
1 tsp	Vegetable oil
2 tsp	Garam masala powder
½ tsp	Salt

In a small bowl mix the nuts with the garam masala.

Heat a non-stick frying pan with the oil.

Add the nuts and heat through for 2 minutes, stirring continually.

Allow to cool then toss in the salt and place in a bowl.

Chef's Note:

- These are great as a snack or to go in a lunch box.

Chapter 12

GI food tables

The food tables below list many common foods and their GI values. The low-GI foods can be eaten freely as they will not significantly raise blood-sugar levels. The medium-GI foods should can be eaten in moderation. The high-GI foods are rapidly digested and absorbed, causing blood sugar levels to rise rapidly. These foods should be avoided.

Food	Low GI (55 or less)	Medium GI (56–69)	High GI (70 or over)	GI value
BEVERAGES				
Fruit Juices				
Apple juice, pure, unsweetened	x			40
Carrot juice	x			43
Grapefruit juice, unsweetened	x			48

Food	Low GI (55 or less)	Medium GI (56–69)	High GI (70 or over)	GI value
Orange juice, unsweetened	×			52
Pineapple juice, unsweetened	×			46
Tomato juice, no added sugar	×			38
Cranberry juice drink		×		56
Soft drinks, sports drinks and milk-based drinks				
Raspberry smoothie	×			33
Banana smoothie	×			30
Yakult, fermented milk drink	×			46
Water	×			0
Coca Cola		×		58
Cordial (added sugar)		×		66
Fanta		×		68
Gatorade			×	78
Isostar			×	70
Lucozade			×	95

Note: although soft drinks like Coca Cola and Fanta are medium GI, they are still not recommended in the diet as they provide nothing else other than energy and are often referred to as 'empty calories'.

Food	Low GI (55 or less)	Medium GI (56–69)	High GI (70 or over)	GI value
BREAKFAST CEREALS				
All-Bran	x			42
Muesli, Alpen	x			55
Muesli, toasted	x			43
Muesli, natural	x			49
Oatmeal	x			55
Just Right		x		60
Muesli, Swiss		x		56
Nutri-Grain		x		66
Porridge		x		58
Porridge, instant		x		66
Raisin Bran		x		61
Sustain		x		68
Bran Flakes			x	74
Cheerios			x	74
Coco Pops			x	77
Corn Flakes			x	81
Corn Pops			x	80
Crunchy Nut Cornflakes			x	72
Honey rice bubbles			x	77
Honey Smacks			x	71
Puffed wheat/ Sugar Puffs			x	74
Rice Krispies			x	87

Food	Low GI (55 or less)	Medium GI (56–69)	High GI (70 or over)	GI value
Shredded Wheat			x	75
Special K			x	84
Sultana Bran			x	73
Weetabix			x	70
Breakfast Bars & Snacks				
Muesli Bar		x		61
Rice Krispies bar		x		63
Crunchy Nut Cornflakes bar			x	72
Fruit winders			x	99
Pop Tarts			x	70
DAIRY PRODUCTS				
Milk, full-fat	x			27
Milk, skimmed	x			32
Soya milk	x			44
Yoghurt	x			36
Yoghurt, low-fat (sugar)	x			33
Yoghurt, low-fat (sweetened)	x			14
Ice cream (regular)		x		61

Food	Low GI (55 or less)	Medium GI (56–69)	High GI (70 or over)	GI value
FRUIT				
Apples	x			38
Apricots, dried	x			31
Banana, unripe	x			30
Cherries	x			22
Fruit cocktail, canned	x			55
Grapefruit	x			25
Grapes, green	x			43
Kiwi	x			53
Mango	x			51
Oranges	x			42
Peach, raw	x			42
Peaches, canned in natural juice	x			38
Pear	x			38
Pears, canned in natural juice	x			43
Plum	x			39
Prunes	x			29
Strawberries, fresh, raw	x			40
Apricots, canned in syrup		x		64
Apricots, raw		x		57

Food	Low GI (55 or less)	Medium GI (56–69)	High GI (70 or over)	GI value
Figs		x		61
Grapes, black		x		59
Peach, canned in syrup		x		58
Pineapple, raw		x		59
Raisins		x		64
Rockmelon / cantaloupe		x		65
Sultanas		x		56
Dates, dried			x	100
Banana, ripe			x	70
Watermelon			x	72
PASTA AND NOODLES				
Fettucine, egg	x			40
Instant noodles	x			46
Linguine, thick, durum	x			46
Linguine, thin durum	x			52
Macaroni	x			47
Ravioli, meat-filled	x			39
Rice noodles, fresh	x			40
Spaghetti, wholemeal	x			37

Food	Low GI (55 or less)	Medium GI (56-69)	High GI (70 or over)	GI value
Spaghetti, white	x			42
Vermicelli, white boiled	x			35
Gnocchi		x		68
Rice noodles, dried		x		61
Spaghetti, canned in tomato sauce		x		68
Udon Noodles, plain		x		62
Rice pasta			x	92
CEREAL GRAINS				
Barley	x			25
Barley, cracked	x			50
Buckwheat	x			54
Oatmeal	x			55
Rice, brown	x			55
Rye, whole kernels	x			34
Wheat, whole kernels	x			41
Wheat, bulgur	x			48
Wheat, semolina	x			55
Barley, rolled		x		66
Cornmeal		x		69
Couscous		x		65
Rice, arborio, risotto, boiled		x		69

Food	Low GI (55 or less)	Medium GI (56–69)	High GI (70 or over)	GI value
Rice, basmati		x		58
Rice, long grain		x		56
Rice, wild		x		57
Millet			x	71
Rice, instant or puffed			x	70
Rice, jasmine			x	100
Rice, white, boiled			x	70
BREADS				
Burgen soya and linseed bread	x			36
Pumpernickel	x			55
Fruit loaf	x			44
Multigrain / Granary bread	x			48
Rye bread	x			50
Wholemeal bread		x		64
Wholewheat sour dough		x		54
White pitta bread		x		57
Bagel, white			x	72
Baguette, white			x	95
Croissant			x	70
Crumpet			x	70

Food	Low GI (55 or less)	Medium GI (56–69)	High GI (70 or over)	GI value
Crusty white bread rolls			×	73
Muffin, plain			×	75
Lebanese bread, white			×	75
Melba toast			×	70
Pikelets			×	85
White bread			×	70
CRACKERS				
Cream cracker		×		65
Rye crispbread		×		64
Wheat cracker		×		67
Plain salted cracker		×		56
Puffed cracker			×	87
Puffed crispbread			×	81
Rice cakes			×	78
Water biscuit			×	71
BEANS, PEAS & NUTS				
Baked beans in tomato sauce	×			48
Black bean	×			20
Black-eyed beans	×			42
Brown beans	×			38

Food	Low GI (55 or less)	Medium GI (56-69)	High GI (70 or over)	GI value
Butter beans	x			31
Chickpeas	x			28
Cashew nuts, unsalted	x			22
Green beans	x			30
Green peas	x			48
Haricot beans	x			38
Hummus	x			6
Kidney beans	x			28
Lentils, green	x			30
Lentils, red	x			26
Lima beans	x			32
Marrowfat peas	x			39
Mung beans	x			38
Peanuts, unsalted	x			14
Pinto beans	x			39
Red beans	x			26
Soya beans	x			18
Split peas,yellow	x			32
VEGETABLES				
Carrots	x			47
Green peas	x			48
Sweet corn	x			54
Yam	x			51
Beetroot		x		64

Food	Low GI (55 or less)	Medium GI (56–69)	High GI (70 or over)	GI value
Potato, canned		×		63
Potato, new, boiled		×		37
Sweet potato		×		61
Broad beans			×	79
Parsnips			×	97
Potato, baked, white			×	85
Potato, boiled, white			×	75
Crisps / French fries			×	75
Potato, mashed			×	74
Potato, instant, mashed			×	85
Swede			×	72
SUGARS				
Fructose (fruit sugar), as an additive	×			19
Lactose	×			46
Honey		×		55
Glucose			×	100
Maltose			×	100
Sucrose (table sugar)			×	70

Food	Low GI (55 or less)	Medium GI (56-69)	High GI (70 or over)	GI value
MIXED MEALS				
Soups				
Lentil	x			44
Minestrone	x			39
Tomato	x			38
Black bean		x		64
Green pea		x		66
Split pea		x		60
Convenience Foods				
Spaghetti Bolognese	x			52
Sushi	x			52
Macaroni Cheese		x		64
Stir fried vegetables, chicken and white rice			x	73
Pizza, cheese and tomato			x	80
Mexican foods				
Pinto beans	x			13
Corn tortilla	x			52
Wheat tortilla	x			30
Taco Shells, cornmeal-based, baked		x		68

Food	Low GI (55 or less)	Medium GI (56–69)	High GI (70 or over)	GI value
Confectionary, cakes and biscuits				
Banana cake		×		55
Digestive biscuits		×		60
Muesli bar with dried fruit		×		61
Muffin, blueberry		×		59
Muffin, bran		×		60
Muffin, carrot		×		62
Oatcakes		×		57
Chocolate and coconut sponge			×	87
Chocolate biscuit			×	73
Doughnuts			×	76
Iced cupcake			×	73
Jelly beans			×	78
Morning coffee biscuits			×	79
Pancakes			×	85
Real fruit bars			×	90
Scones			×	92
Skittles			×	70
Waffles			×	76

Food	Low GI (55 or less)	Medium GI (56-69)	High GI (70 or over)	GI value
Snack foods				
Corn chips, plain, salted	x			43
Rice and corn snacks			x	74
Popcorn			x	72
Pretzels			x	83
MISCELLANEOUS				
Marmalade	x			48
Strawberry jam		x		51
Paxo bread stuffing			x	74

All values taken from: Foster-Powell K, Holt S.H.A, Brand-Miller C.B. International table of glycemic index and glycemic load values: 2002. *American Journal of clinical Nutrition*. 2002; 76:5-56.

New products are being assessed all the time. For new additions refer to: www.glycemicindex.com and search the database.

Part Three

Physical Activity

Chapter 13

Why exercise is important

The word 'exercise' can bring back memories of suffering, profuse sweating, aching muscles and even feelings of embarrassment. However, exercise or any physical activity is an essential part of a healthy lifestyle. I hated exercise when I was growing up and blame my childhood weight problem on my lack of physical activity during childhood. Like many children, I would conjure up elaborate plans to avoid PE at school, and the idea of doing exercise at home, such as going for a run or playing football in the garden, was something I abhored. The lack of exercise led to a spiral of decreasing fitness and increasing feelings of inadequacy, as most young boys are judged by their peers on their physical prowess. The more unfit I became, the less confident I felt, the more I ate and the more the weight piled on. This additional weight caused problems with the joints in my legs and feet.

My doctor referred me for physiotherapy and to a podiatrist

to try to correct the problem. The physiotherapist told us that not all types of exercise were suitable for me and that, owing to my weight, certain sports, such as running, actually did me more harm than good. Pursuits such as swimming or cycling would be much more suitable, improving my fitness while not putting my body under too much stress.

However, I had first to conquer my dislike and fear of exercise. With the help of my parents, I started finding out what types of sports or activity classes were available in the area. I joined a karate class and went for swimming lessons. My parents also bought a trampoline for me to use in the garden. This would keep me entertained and active for hours on end. Getting fit is a slow, steady process, but one that reaps countless rewards.

When I reached university I learnt that dieting was not advised for children and teenagers but that by increasing my activity levels and burning more energy, my body would start to use up its fat stores and also build muscle tissue, which would increase my metabolism. I became much more confident within myself, which was noticed by family and friends. I used to sweat a lot, which made me feel uncomfortable in social settings. But as my fitness improved and my weight stabilised, I found that I would sweat a lot less. My exercise-induced wheezing and asthma improved dramatically and, before long, I had no symptoms at all. I was less anxious in general, as exercise helped release a lot of pent-up fears and frustration, and I was much happier overall. These are just a few personal examples of the benefits that improving fitness can reap.

When you are unfit, exercise can be quite an ordeal for one's body and often leaves you feeling stiff and sore for a few days. The reason for this is that you often overdo it the first few times you exercise after long periods of abstinence. Thankfully, after many failed attempts, I discovered that the secret is to start off very slowly and increase gradually so that the body adapts to the extra work, making it less painful during – as well as after – the exercise. Even if you only exercise for five to ten minutes and enjoy it, that is a lot better than slogging it out for longer and feeling awful the next day.

Another preconception is that exercise has to involve going to the gym or running a marathon. This is not true. Exercise can be as simple as walking to work and back every day, using the stairs instead of the lift, or getting off the bus a few stops short of your destination. I have found that when I am too busy with work, or just not motivated to go to the gym, that walking to work and back daily has helped me to maintain a healthy weight and has made incorporating exercise into my daily routine a reality for me.

In this section I will point out why it is so important to keep the body working well and show you easy ways to motivate your children to becoming more active. Children, by nature, love anything fun, so instead of forcing them to get fit through rigorous, structured exercise routines, I will show you how to use games and everyday routines to increase their activity levels. I will also suggest ways for the whole family to enjoy living an active lifestyle, with lots of activities to do in your free time in the evenings and at the weekends, enjoying fun-filled, active pastimes together. It is important to note that children learn by example and so you will have to set a good example in order to show your children that exercise is an important and enjoyable part of a healthy lifestyle. If you start incorporating activity into your daily routine, they are much more likely to follow suit.

The benefits of exercise

Exercise has many health and psychological benefits, and can even help family dynamics and relationships if carried out as a family unit. The most important benefit is that exercise burns up excessive energy that would otherwise be stored as fat. A good way to think about it – and a way that often helps me – is that if you exercise and burn up energy you can be more relaxed about the foods you eat, as a normal intake will not lead to weight gain. If you are very inactive, even normal amounts of food can lead to weight gain. Many people think you only burn up the number of calories that is shown on the treadmill or exercise bike. In fact, exercise raises your metabolism for many hours afterwards, continuing the energy-burning process.

Exercise not only increases the energy you burn but it also makes you feel good. Exercise causes your body to produce the neurotransmitter (brain messenger chemical) serotonin, which leads to improved mood and feelings of well-being. We have all experienced the emotional 'high' you get following a good bout of physical activity. This 'high' can help to beat depression and make you feel good about yourself and the way you look. It is a great way to improve self-esteem and to increase confidence.

Did you know?

Many people who suffer depression have found that regular physical activity improves their mood and decreases their need for medication.

Children have loads of energy that they need to expend. This energy can be used up in negative ways, such as temper tantrums, causing havoc, or being hyperactive, or it can be harnessed to do fun, safe, physical activities.

Benefits of regular physical activity

- Controls weight: Physical activity by itself can cause modest weight loss of around 0.5kg–1kg per month. However, the best way to lose weight is to combine physical activity with a healthy diet. Remember, if you are doing lots of exercise, your weight on the scales may not be the most accurate indicator of weight loss because the more exercise you do, especially weight (or 'resistance') training, the more muscle you build. See a dietitian or find out whether your local health centre or gym can measure your body fat using skinfold callipers, or a bio-electrical impedance analysis machine (which measures body fat using harmless electrical currents). Your body-fat levels are far more important for your health than the weight shown on the scales. Regular physical activity can help prevent your child becoming just another statistic in the childhood obesity epidemic.

- Prevents high blood pressure: Eighty per cent of obese adolescents have high blood pressure, which can lead to heart disease and stroke in adulthood. Encourage regular short bouts of physical activity to reduce the risk of this.
- Reduces risk of heart disease: This is not usually a disease that children develop but there is growing evidence that the foundations of heart disease can start in childhood, especially if your child is obese and inactive. Being physically inactive and unfit is as big a risk for heart disease as smoking. If you are inactive and unfit, your risk of dying from heart disease is double that of someone who is active and fit.
- Reduces risk of type II diabetes: The prevalence of this problem is increasing in children and adolescents in the UK, although the numbers are still small. Being unfit, inactive and obese are major risk factors for developing type II diabetes. Adults who are active will have a 33–50 per cent lower risk of developing it. If you have a family history of developing diabetes, then you can substantially reduce this risk by encouraging your whole family to be active. If you already have type II diabetes, then being active can help you to manage the condition and also reduce your risk of premature death.

Did you know?

Physically active adults have a 20-30 per cent reduced risk of premature death, and up to 50 per cent reduced risk of developing heart disease, diabetes, stroke and cancer.

Did you know?

There are many pills and potions on the market that claim to raise your metabolism, but the only healthy method is to exercise. Exercise builds muscles, which use energy all the time, even when at rest, so the more muscle you have, the higher your metabolism will be, and the more calories you burn up.

- Improves bone health: Physical activity increases bone strength in teenagers, maintains it in young adults and slows its decline in old age. The greatest benefit to bones occurs early in puberty. Activities such as rambling, hill walking, gymnastics, volleyball, racquet sports, football and mountain-biking may be particularly effective for strengthening bones. Being active can slow down the development of osteoporosis by reducing the rate of bone loss from the late twenties onwards, but it can't reverse advanced bone loss. So it's important to be active from a young age and continue throughout your life. There is also some evidence that being physically active can delay the onset of lower back pain.
- Reduces risk of cancer: Being active reduces your risk of developing cancer. After the menopause physical activity can reduce your risk of developing breast cancer.
- Increases overall psychological well-being: If you lead an active lifestyle you have a reduced risk of suffering from depression. Physical activity is also an effective treatment of mild, moderate and severe clinical depression. If you or your

child feels down and depressed, try incorporating physical activity into your daily routines. It improves mood, reduces anxiety and makes you feel better about yourself. Physical activity also helps combat stress and improves sleep.

- Other benefits: Participation in exercise and sports has been shown to reduce delinquent behaviour and boost academic performance. It helps children learn social skills, such as taking turns, winning, losing and how to be a good sport. It helps them to develop hand-eye coordination, balance and ball skills, and it gives children a sense of camaraderie when playing organised team activities. Best of all, it is a good way for families to enjoy doing fun things together.

How active does my child need to be?

Children and young people should do at least 60 minutes of at least moderately intense physical activity every day. At least twice a week this should include activities to strengthen bones, muscle strength and flexibility.

How active do adults need to be?

For general health benefits, adults should do at least moderately intense physical activity on five or more days of the week for at

Did you know?

In England, walking is still the most common form of physical activity but, along with cycling, has declined by 26 per cent.

Did you know?

Twenty per cent of boys and girls between the ages of two and 15 do less than 30 minutes of physical activity per day. Two-thirds of men and three-quarters of women do less than 30 minutes of moderately intense physical activity a day on at least five days per week.

least 30 minutes a day. To increase weight loss, you will need to do 45–60 minutes of moderately intense physical activity per day.

You don't have to go to the gym to achieve the recommended levels of activity listed. In fact, activities that are part of everyday life such as briskly walking to work, shops or school, climbing stairs, and cycling are all moderately intense physical activities and count towards your quota for the day. Also, you do not have to do 30 minutes all in one go. Shorter bouts of exercise of at least 10–15 minutes a few times a day are just as good.

How to achieve the recommended levels of physical activity

Young child

- Daily walk to and from school.
- Daily school activity sessions (breaks and clubs).
- 3–4 afternoon or evening play opportunities.
- Weekend: longer walks, visits to park or swimming pool, bike rides.

Teenager

- Daily walk (or cycle) to and from school.
- 3–4 organised or informal midweek sports or activities.
- Weekend: longer walks, biking, swimming, sports activities.

Student

- Daily walk (or cycle) to and from college.
- Taking all opportunities to be active: using stairs, doing manual tasks, and so on.
- 2–3 midweek sport, gym, or swimming sessions.
- Weekend: longer walks, cycling, swimming, sports activities.

Adult – employed

- Daily walk (or cycle) to and from work.
- Taking all opportunities to be active: using stairs, doing manual tasks, and so on.
- 2–3 midweek sport, gym, or swimming sessions.
- Weekend: longer walks, cycling, swimming, sports activities, DIY, gardening.

Adult – houseworker

- Daily walks, gardening or DIY.
- Taking all opportunities to be active: using stairs, doing manual tasks, and so on.
- Occasional midweek sport, gym, or swimming sessions.
- Weekend: longer walks, cycling, sports activities.

Adult – unemployed

- Daily walks, gardening, DIY.
- Taking all opportunities to be active: using stairs, doing manual tasks, and so on.
- Weekend: longer walks, cycling, swimming, or sports activities.
- Occasional sport, gym, or swimming sessions.

Retired person

- Daily walks, cycling, DIY or gardening.
- Taking all opportunities to be active: using stairs, doing manual tasks.
- Weekend: longer walks, cycling or swimming.

Source: Department of Health 2004.

You don't have to be thin to be healthy

Overweight and even obese children and adults can still get fit, no matter what their weight, and getting fit will improve your health. Studies have shown that overweight people who are unfit have much higher levels of disease than those of the same weight who are fit. For some adults, accepting that they are never going to be the size they were when they left school but that they can still be fit and healthy can be an important realisation. We should all strive to get fit, no matter what we weigh.

Why are some children not active enough?

All healthy children are physically active when they are young, and encouraging them to do so is not really an issue. Generally, as kids get older, however, their main outlet for exercise takes place at school. Over the last decade or so, sport at school has slowly taken a back seat to academic demands. The growing pressure on schools to achieve high academic grades has meant that time spent on Physical Education (PE) during school has decreased.

One PE session a week is definitely not enough to meet a child's physical activity needs. For many children, this may be the only time they do exercise. Also, as the school day has got longer and longer, the amount of after-school sports time has significantly decreased. Children also have increasing amounts of homework, and so time left for active play and sports has sharply declined. Another factor is that PE at school has traditionally been centred around team sports such as cricket, rugby, football, netball and hockey. These sports are competitive by nature and involve winners and losers. Finding yourself on the losing side time after time can damage a child's self-esteem and confidence. As far as children are concerned, what their peers think of them is of foremost importance. Being popular and respected is crucial to a happy school life. Sports prowess can make or break a child's acceptance, especially amongst boys. Girls often find their changing body shape a source of embarrassment and will find excuses to avoid wearing revealing swimming costumes in front of the boys.

PE is designed for healthy, fit kids and often little is done to make sure that children of lower fitness and ability levels are included and able to play to the best of their abilities. If I think back to my years of PE, much of the time was spent waiting for my turn to hit/kick/throw/catch the ball and I was, in fact, quite sedentary. Children can spend as little as eight minutes exercising at the required intensity during a 45 minute-long PE class. Traditionally, PE has not been designed for the one in five children who is now overweight. Children do not necessarily have to play competitive team sports in order to keep fit. Other activities that promote fitness, such as martial arts or dance, should be encouraged. These activities should be fun and inclusive, otherwise we risk a generation of adults with negative childhood memories of exercise. Activities that are fun and non-competitive and introduced early on will encourage an enjoyment for physical activity. On the opposite side of the coin, some children are scared of doing sport for fear of failure or stress from overly-pushy parents. Excessive pressure on young children can do more harm than good in many cases. Exercise and sport should be fun and enjoyable so that children enjoy being active and are more likely to grow up to become active adults who enjoy exercising.

Case study – puberty

Mary loved swimming: the crawl was her favourite stroke. She was the second fastest girl in her year and took great pride in this fact. She loved going to swimming practice and enjoyed the fact that her coach took special interest in her above the other children. However, things changed when Mary, aged 11, had her first period and had begun to develop breasts. Being the first of her schoolmates to reach puberty made her feel awkward, embarrassed and extremely self-conscious. She began to develop a phobia that her period would strike while swimming. She was also embarrassed of the growing attention her breasts were drawing from the older boys at her school. She began to complain of tummy aches to get out of swimming practice and refused to try out for the school team. Her parents were extremely disappointed but accepted her decision and did not push her.

Mary's lifestyle took a dramatic change: instead of going swimming three times a week after school she now went straight home, changed into her brother's loose hand-me-down jumpers and baggy tracksuit bottoms and lay in front of the television munching her favourite sweets and crisps. As her body was developing at a rapid rate her appetite began to increase and she was constantly hungry so she started eating even more junk food and sweets. Her mum was not home in the afternoons to supervise what she ate and to keep her company and most of her friends were busy with their own afternoon activities, so food became her only companion.

Mary began to put on excess weight. By the time Mary reached her 12th birthday she had put on 4kg of excess weight and could not fit into her jeans. Her dad suggested she ate less junk food, which made her even more uncomfortable. She wore looser clothing to hide her shape and rebelled by eating even more sweets and crisps. Her mum bought ready-made healthy meals for Mary, but she refused to eat them, saying she wanted what the rest of the family was eating. So her mum went to see the GP for advice and the family was referred to me for a consultation. When I saw Mary with her parents my impression was that she was a very angry child, who was ashamed of her appearance. I asked her parents to leave the room and enquired of Mary how she felt I could help her. She confided that she was embarrassed about her body and wanted to lose weight, as her breasts were even larger now she had begun putting on weight. I explained the principles of eating low-GI foods and how they would fill her up for longer periods of time and give her more energy. I also told her that exercise was crucial to her feeling good and healthy and recommended that she find another afternoon activity to replace swimming – one which did not involve having to show her body. She said she liked hockey and wouldn't mind giving that a go. She said she would try to cut out junk food and go to two hockey practices a week. On the days that she went straight home she agreed to limit television to just one or two of her favourite programmes in the afternoon and eat only healthy treats such as frozen yoghurts and home-made smoothies. I then had a private discussion with her parents asking them to look at their own eating and exercise patterns and try to be role models for Mary. They said the whole family would try eating the foods I had recommended for Mary and at the weekends they would do fun active things together, like cycling in their local park.

A few months later, I received a hand-written 'thank-you' card from Mary, in which she said that she was feeling much better about herself. She had lost a kilo and was no longer feeling so self conscious. She also said that her new diet gave her more strength and stamina and that she had been asked to play for the school hockey team. However, she was also considering taking up swimming again. Mary's case shows that to deal with overweight kids you have to look at their lifestyle habits and their emotional state, and not just focus on what they eat.

Television – friend or foe?

The television has become an indispensable part of our lives. Many homes have one in the main living area as well as in the bedrooms. It is used to keep children company, to baby-sit and to help them fall asleep. Some children watch up to six hours of television per day during the week and even more at the weekends. In addition there is the time spent on computer games and the Internet, all adding up to a big part of children's lives. The problem is that time spent watching television is time spent being inactive. Children go into an almost coma-like state when watching television and use up even less energy than reading a book! Often television watching is accompanied by snacking of inappropriate foods. Studies have shown that food eaten in this situation leads to more calories being consumed than if food was eaten without distractions.

Another important issue is television advertising and whether this has an influence on the types of foods children are eating. The majority of food and drink advertisements shown during the hours that children most often watch TV are for food products that are high in fat, sugar and salt. Could this be contributing to their insatiable appetite for unhealthy foods? Research has shown that children are influenced by what they

Did you know?

The greatest consumption of snacks occurs while children are watching television.

see on television and so the government is becoming concerned about advertisements for unhealthy foods shown during children's television hours.

Kick their television habit fast

There are far better ways for kids to pass their time than watching television. Draw on your own experiences as a child. What did you do to have fun? You will be amazed at the enjoyment your kids will get from playing old-time favourites, like hopscotch and Twister.

Alternatives to television

- Make a list of your child's favourite programmes and limit their viewing time to these.
- Keep the television switched off at all other times.
- Play fun active games with your children during the times they would usually spend in front of the television.
- Leave activity-based games lying around to entice them away from the television, such as skipping ropes, hula hoops, and soccer balls.
- Introduce your children to a craft or hobby they can do at home such as painting, model-making, sewing or collecting.

- Help them access hidden interests or talents instead of being couch potatoes.
- Learn another language with your children.
- Instead of the whole family watching evening television, play a family game, such as cards or board games.

How can I get my kids to be more active?

Children love to play, so encourage them to do other activities that involve moving around. Any form of physical activity will burn more energy than sitting in front of the television or computer.

There are many ways you can encourage your kids to be more active. Ideally, if you can encourage them to be active on their own some days and to do things with you on the other days, you will not only be building stronger family bonds but also getting fit yourself. It is really important that you set a good example. Here are some ideas:

- Be firm: make a rule and stick to it. Restrict television watching to 1–2 hours per day, including playing computer games and using the Internet. (Occasionally, they may need to use the Internet for school work but still restrict the time to one hour maximum at one sitting and then get them to take an activity break.) Ask your kids to choose their favourite programmes and only let them watch these.
- Spend time playing active games with your children such as kicking a ball, basketball hoops, Twister, hopscotch, skipping or hide and seek. Set a good example. Playing active games together is not only fun but counts as physical activity for the whole family.

- Make sure that physical activities are seen as a reward and not a punishment, then your kids will be more likely to join in and enjoy themselves. If you have bad memories of exercise yourself, rid your mind of these notions and start afresh.
- If your kids refuse to join in at first, don't let it stop you doing physical activities. Make sure they see the positive effects they have on you. You can also use personalities they look up to, such as pop singers or sports stars, to demonstrate what keeping fit and strong can achieve.
- Don't hold your kids back. Give them every opportunity to partake in physical activities and games. Find out what is available at your local leisure centre or community hall, present the options to your kids and allow them to decide what they would enjoy. If they are reluctant to try, ask them just to give it a go. Speak to the class leader in advance, explaining that you are trying to encourage them to be more active and ask them to make sure your children enjoy their first class, thereby increasing the likelihood that they will continue attending.
- Don't expect you or your kids to go from couch potato to marathon runner overnight. Start with small bouts of activity you enjoy, and gradually increase the length and intensity. A short walk to the park with your dog, or throwing a Frisbee for 10 minutes, is a good start. Everyday activities like riding a bike, playing outside, or helping with the housework should be encouraged as they promote getting up and moving instead of sitting and being inactive.
- If you have a teenager who is refusing to do any sport, speak

to other parents to find out about after-school activities, such as martial arts, gymnastics, swimming, dance classes, yoga or even aerobics. Your children may not even be aware that such activities exist.

- Organise family picnics or trips to parks or any open space

Taking steps

A good way to measure your family's activity levels is to buy them all a pedometer. This can be worn on a belt and measures the number of steps you take. Encourage them to wear it every day. Make a chart showing the days of the week and the names of all family members and write down the number of steps you all take daily. Make sure that the winner receives a prize or a special treat, such as a trip to the amusement park, or a new football kit.

In healthy adults:

- Less than 5,000 steps per day is considered sedentary. From 5,000–7,500 steps is considered low-active. From 7,500–10,000 steps is medium-active. From 10,000–12,500 is active. Above 12,500 is highly active.
- Taking 4,000 steps equals approximately 30 minutes of moderately intense walking, while 10,000 steps requires between 45 and 60 minutes of serious walking per day.
- When starting to become more active, aim for 3,000 more steps than you usually do. So, for example, if you usually do 4,000 steps, aim for 7,000 and gradually build it up.

where you can kick a ball around or play other active games with your children.

- Walk and cycle with your children instead of using the car. Find out if there are any safe cycle routes near your home and use these whenever possible (check www.sustrans.org.uk). Walk whenever possible – it's a great form of exercise.
- Keep an eye on your children. Watch for signs of boredom or excessive time being sedentary and suggest activities to keep them busy.
- If you are too tired or busy to be active with your children, then invite one of their friends around to keep them company. Do not allow them to just sit in front of the television or computer. Encourage them to do something active.

Case study – exercise

Edna grew up in the country as one of seven children. Her parents ran the local bakery and always brought home baked delicacies such as jam doughnuts, cheesecakes and pastries. All the children loved to feast on their parents' goodies. *Edna's brothers and sisters all shared a passion for horse riding, which helped them maintain a healthy weight. Edna hated being outdoors and preferred to spend her time indoors reading and writing. Edna grew to weigh more than her three older sisters and needed to wear larger clothes sizes.*

When Edna came down with 'flu and was taken to the local GP, her doctor said she was more worried about Edna's weight, suggesting that she begin exercising to help her slim down. Her parents forced her to join her eldest brother (a natural-born athlete) every morning before school for a run around the local farmland. She was forced to endure these morning runs throughout her school years, leaving her with an extreme dislike for any form of physical activity – especially running.

As an adult, Edna managed to maintain a healthy weight. Unfortunately her own daughter, Jessica, who was 15, developed a weight problem herself. Jessica was referred to me by her GP and brought in for a consultation. Her weight put her in the obese category and her waist circumference put her in the high-risk category. Her GP had said she had high blood pressure and was suffering from mild sleep apnoea, which is a difficulty breathing during sleep. This causes the sufferer to wake up during sleep. It also starves the brain of oxygen, leaving the sufferer feeling tired the following day. The problem, according to Edna, was that Jessica spent all her pocket money on snacks, that the kids considered to be 'cool'. Children who had fruit, vegetables and brown bread in their lunch boxes were sometimes teased, according to Jessica. She always begged her mother to buy the latest lunch box 'fad foods'. By the time Jessica returned home from school in the afternoons, she was so full that she refused to eat the healthy food that Edna prepared for her dinner. Edna never tried to get her daughter to do anything active because she remembered how much she had hated it as a little girl. Instead, Edna tried to make Jessica stop snacking and eat the meals she had prepared for her, but the constant junk food advertising, peer-group pressure, and Jessica's love of sweet food made this impossible. Edna felt she was fighting a losing battle.

I asked them to keep a three-day food diary and note all the physical activity that Jessica did. Analysis of the food diary revealed a diet high in calories, fat and sugar, and low in fruit and vegetables. The physical activity diary showed that Jessica was very inactive and was doing far less than the prescribed amount of exercise for her age. She was driven to school and picked up every day in the car and did not participate in any sport whatsoever. I could tell from the food diary that Edna knew quite a bit about healthy eating. She had already replaced full-fat cheese, yoghurt and milk with low-fat versions and had begun serving baked fish with rice instead of making fried fish and chip dinners. I commended her on trying to improve the family nutrition, emphasising to Jessica that it was not only aimed at her but that her mother wanted the whole family to be healthier. I asked Jessica if she would like to feel healthier, she said 'yes' but said she hated to be teased about bringing healthy food to school. Her mum added that all of Jessica's friends were large girls. After discussing things for a while, Jessica realised that her friends were only teasing her because they would feel jealous if she lost weight. I told her they might be more understanding if she explained that she needed to lose weight because of her health. She said she would try. Jessica preferred snacking to eating meals, so I asked her mum to stop trying to make her eat three meals a day and allow her to snack on healthy low-GI foods. I gave her mother a long list of sweet, low-fat and low-GI goodies that she could keep in the house for Jessica to snack on. Jessica was attentive and seemed willing to give up the junk food. However the hard work was yet to begin.

It was essential that Jessica begin to include some form of physical activity into her daily routine. The easiest way to get Jessica to become more active was for her to see her mother doing it. But first I needed to find a way to combat Edna's aversion to exercise. I asked Edna about her daily chores and her favourite pastimes. She replied that her days were largely taken up with getting her kids off to school, writing for the local community newspaper, grocery shopping, and preparing dinner. Any spare time she had was spent reading and pottering around in the garden.

Next we looked at Jessica's routine. She liked staying indoors and kept herself entertained by chatting to her American and Australian pen pals via the Internet and doing her homework. She said that most of her friends were too busy in the afternoons playing hockey to come over and she did not enjoy playing sport. However, she loved playing Monopoly, family card games and Scrabble. The family often played games on Saturday mornings and on rainy days.

I realised from this that the family enjoyed spending time together, so I suggested that they try to include fun, active pursuits such as hopscotch, egg and spoon races, Twister, dance competitions, mystery walks, treasure hunts and swimming, which Edna said they all liked to do – especially on holidays. I also asked Jessica to walk home from school every day with some of her friends who lived close by. I suggested that Edna could take Jessica to her favourite bookshop to buy a new book as a reward, at least once a week. Jessica was excited by this as she loved buying books, which were normally only an occasional treat. I tried to incorporate physical activity into their everyday lifestyle, rather that trying to suggest that they take up a rigid exercise routine.

I saw Jessica every week for three months and then monthly for eight months. In this time, she slowly began to increase her activity levels. Edna even started walking Jessica to school every day so that they would both gain the benefits of being more active. They both realised that the more walking they did, the better they felt generally. Combined with the healthy diet they were following, Jessica began to lose a bit of weight. Although she still fell in the obese category, Jessica was much fitter and her blood pressure had returned to normal. The sleep apnoea was considerably better too, and she was now noticeably more alert during the day and managing to achieve better marks in her exams.

Part Four

Changing Behaviour

Chapter 14

Improving self-esteem and confidence

Improving your family's health involves more than learning about nutrition and activity levels, it is also about swapping unhealthy, ingrained behaviour patterns for healthier ones. One of the main reasons that many people fail to make significant long-term changes to their lifestyle is that they don't deal with the underlying factors that cause them to overeat and avoid exercise in the first place, making it very difficult to maintain a healthy long-term diet and exercise regime. For example, depression, low self-esteem or lack of confidence may all contribute to overeating and lack of physical activity. I will show you how you can identify what may be triggering these problems and how to use simple techniques to achieve changes in the way your children view themselves. How often do you eat because you are feeling bored or have had a stressful day? A lot of the time we eat as a way to comfort ourselves. The following section contains many useful techniques, such as a goal-and-reward system, healthy triggers and role modelling to improve your own and your children's relationship with food.

Just as being depressed can lead to overweight, so being overweight can lead to depression and create a vicious circle where the more depressed you become the more you overeat – leading to more depression. Overweight and obese children often have low self-esteem and confidence. Many are bullied and taunted at school, all of which compounds their feelings of inadequacy and poor self-worth. For some, these long-term psychological effects can be worse than the harmful medical effects of being overweight. Being an overweight or obese child can leave deep, often permanent psychological scars. As an overweight child, I was constantly being told by my parents and teachers that I should try to lose some weight and reminded of what I should and shouldn't eat. Unfortunately what they didn't realise was that their comments only served to further reduce my self-esteem and increase my feelings of inadequacy. This shows how sensitive overweight children can be and why parents should not focus on these things.

I know for myself that long after I had stopped being classified as obese, I still felt fat, no matter what the scales or my peers told me. No matter how many times you are told that you look good or slim, unless you actually believe it yourself, you will never overcome feeling like a fat person trapped in a thin person's body. I also know from many conversations with healthy-weight adults who were overweight as children that they have been left with permanent psychological scars. To my mind, one of the most important reasons for helping to prevent children becoming overweight is to keep them from a lifetime of feeling unhappy with their bodies and lacking confidence. If children are already overweight, there are many things that parents can do to help raise their self-esteem and make them feel good about themselves. Being a parent of an unhappy child is extremely difficult, and so I am going to give you lots of suggestions and ideas on improving your children's self-esteem and confidence.

How to tell if your child is depressed

Here are some signs and symptoms of depression:

- Often sad, tearful or cries a lot.
- Less interested in activities.
- Does not enjoy previous favourite pastimes.
- Always bored.
- Has low energy levels.
- Socially isolated and a poor communicator.
- Low self-esteem.
- Very sensitive towards rejection or failure.
- Often irritable, angry or even hostile.
- Problems with relationships.
- Often complains of physical illness, such as headaches and stomach aches.
- Often misses school.
- Under-achieving at school.
- Poor concentration.
- Changes in eating and/or sleeping patterns.
- Talks about, or has tried, running away from home.

Did you know?

The longer children remain overweight, the more they are at risk of depression and other mental health disorders.

- Talks about, or has tried, committing suicide (or other self-destructive behaviour).

If you notice any of these signs and you are worried that your child might be depressed, make an appointment with a mental health professional or your family GP for evaluation and diagnosis.

Dos and don'ts of improving self-esteem and confidence in your children

- Do praise children for accomplishments and for effort.
- Do use words of encouragement such as 'well done', 'that's great', 'how clever you are' wherever possible.
- Do encourage your children in whatever interests them, even if you think it's uninteresting or a waste of time.
- Do allow them to wear whatever they want, thereby allowing them to feel comfortable with their appearance. What you think is fashionable is probably very different from what is 'in' with their peer group.
- Do teach your children positive self-statements. If you notice

your children making a negative statement about themselves, such as 'I can't do anything right', or 'I'm so stupid', then correct them by restating the comment in a more positive way. For example, say, 'You made a mistake this time but next time you will get it right'.

- Do teach your children to make their own decisions and to take responsibility for their own mistakes and successes. Point out to them when they have made a good decision and allow them to solve their own problems, which will give them confidence in themselves. Answer their questions and help them to think of alternative options.
- Do treat all your children the same. Do not allow a normal weight child to have 'treats' while an overweight child is forced to eat salad. Encourage the whole family to eat healthy foods, and exercise together.
- Do learn to laugh at your own mistakes. This will teach your children that life doesn't have to be serious all the time.
- Do remember to focus on health and not appearance.
- Do regularly tell your children that you love them and always will.
- Do make time to play with your children, no matter what their ages. Sharing a hobby or going to a sports match together will strengthen your relationship. This will increase the likelihood that they will share their concerns and worries with you and seek your advice.
- Do teach by example. Remember to radiate a positive self-esteem, and never put yourself down.
- Do encourage your children to set high but realistic goals.

Setting unrealistic goals will only set them up for failure.

- Don't force your children to take part in sports or exercises that they don't enjoy. Rather, encourage them to take part in sports and exercises that they like and feel confident about.
- Don't make fun of your children's feelings or insecurities.
- Don't comment only on bad behaviour and take good behaviour for granted.
- Don't compare siblings or encourage them to compete. Make sure that you give equal attention to all.
- Don't show favouritism to one child, this can be detrimental to all.
- Don't call your children names such as 'chubby', 'lazy', 'plump', 'big'. By labelling your child, you can undermine their confidence. Teasing or embarrassing a child will only make things worse.
- Don't demand perfection from your children, none of us is perfect.
- Don't criticise your child for doing something bad, instead criticise the bad act.

Case study – negative talk

When Claudia's father came to see me, he was very worried about his 16-year-old daughter's health – not only her physical size but also her relationship with her mother. He confided in me that Claudia felt really bad about herself, as she could never live up to her mother's standards. His wife had been a ballerina in her youth and had a naturally developed, toned and petite figure and had wanted a daughter who took after her. Unfortunately, much to her disappointment, Claudia had inherited her father's rounded shoulders and heavy-set frame. Claudia had not been fat as a child but had always been classed as 'a large girl'. Her father said that Claudia felt she was a constant source of shame to her mother and so turned to food for comfort.

Slowly she began putting on weight and prematurely grew out of her clothes. Claudia's furious mum had taken her daughter to a diet club, even though her father had opposed this. Claudia was instructed on what food to eat, how much and when. Her mother now watched Claudia like a hawk and often made disparaging remarks, telling her she was disgusting for eating so much and that no boys would ever look at her. Claudia would feel worse about herself and she would compensate by eating more and more, mostly behind her mother's back. Claudia's father got in touch with me and I suggested he speak to his wife and set up an appointment to come and see me. He did not attend the initial consultation because of work commitments and so Claudia and her mother came on their own. Sitting in my office, Claudia's mother said that her daughter was fat, unattractive and unpopular and that she had absolutely no will-power and never stuck to any diets and that I was the last hope. Before any more was said, I asked Claudia to leave the room so that I could have a word with her mother alone. I asked her if she had ever heard of the concept of positive re-enforcement, she admitted that she hadn't. I explained to her that what Claudia needed was not only a modification of her diet and behaviour towards food but that she also needed supportive and positive parents who would help give her confidence in herself. Without allowing my dismay to show, I said that negative talk was severely damaging her self-confidence along with any chances of developing healthier eating patterns. I asked Claudia's mother what she wanted for her daughter. She responded that she regarded her daughter's size as a poor reflection on her as a mother. She said it hurt her when friends said unkind words about her daughter. I told her that my job was not to make her daughter look good enough for her friends but rather to ensure she was healthy and receiving the right nutrition and support from her family. I said I would treat Claudia only if she and her husband agreed to meet a counsellor to discuss how to improve their familial relationships and parenting skills. She agreed.

Although I knew there were deeper issues to be resolved, I thought we could start by focusing on changing the negative talk. I asked Claudia's mother to agree that, for one week, she would say only positive, loving and encouraging words to her daughter, especially in regard to her weight. I asked her to think of 10 good qualities about her daughter. From these we compiled a list of statements she could say to encourage her daughter. These were some of the things we came up with:

- *I know you have strong willpower and can do anything you set your mind to.*
- *This new food tastes great, I am so happy we have this chance to get healthier together as a family.*
- *Wow, Claudia, you look so healthy and pretty today. Your skin is glowing.*

I also asked Claudia's mother if she was prepared to see this new eating plan as a chance for her whole family, including her two younger children, to get healthy. I told her it was not appropriate to isolate Claudia and put her on a diet as this would seem like a punishment. She said they would all try to eat these new foods together, and she would try to stop her sons eating so much junk food. She also said she was prepared to store all the sweets in a locked cupboard so that Claudia and the boys would only be able to choose healthy food. She was concerned about her daughter's secret snack eating and said she often scolded her for this. I said, instead of shouting at her, that perhaps it would be a better idea to start spending more time with her daughter so that she would feel more loved. Then perhaps the comfort eating would diminish. I warned her that if things did not change her daughter could develop a long-term eating disorder. She admitted that she had once suffered from bulimia while trying to keep her weight down for dancing and also said her mother had been very hard on her. She knew she was being unfair to Claudia and promised to try to be more positive and tolerant.

We called Claudia back into the office and her mother told her that she was proud of her and loved her very much and that 'the whole family was going to try to get healthier together'. I began discussing with Claudia how these new foods would give her energy and help her concentrate better at school. I pointed out that lots of children get sick because of poor nutrition and that she was being given a really special present. By the time she left my office, she seemed happier and saw that this was not a punishment but an opportunity for change.

A few months later I received an email from Claudia saying 'thank you' for making her mum change and that she was happier and had managed to lose weight. Her grades had improved, too, because she was not so sad all the time. The family also attended a course of counselling.

This case, although extreme, highlights the importance of positive talking. Negative talk and fault-finding is detrimental to your children's self-esteem and stunts their emotional growth. Positive talk is a really special gift, and one that we should give all children from a very young age.

Changing unhealthy forms of behaviour into healthy ones

Habits can be healthy or unhealthy. Having something sugary to eat after dinner while watching the television is an example of an unhealthy habit. Taking the dog for a walk is an example of a healthy one. The reason that most diets don't work in the long term is that they do not encourage long-term behaviour changes. Once people stop following the dietary advice they revert to their previous habits. If diets could change people's behaviour permanently, we would see many more long-term success stories. In order to stay on the right path, unhealthy habits need to be transformed into healthier ones.

Unfortunately, a few bad habits can undo a lot of positive hard work. For example, having a chocolate binge every day on the way home from school or work can undo a lot of the benefits of healthy eating the rest of the day. Some people wonder why they can't lose weight when they follow a diet. The reason is that although they follow the diet 90 per cent of the time, the other 10 per cent can undo all the good they have achieved. Eating an unhealthy snack every time you walk past the kitchen cupboard will surely undo any good done eating healthy food at mealtimes. Often these unhealthy habits or routines are done almost automatically and not even remembered. When asking clients what they had eaten in the previous 24 hours, often it is not until I really probe deeper that the few biscuits, sweets or sugary drinks they'd consumed were suddenly recalled to mind. It may be that they were embarrassed, or felt guilty to admit to a dietitian what they actually ate, but in many cases, I believe, people just did not recall eating or drinking these foods as it was pure habit.

So how do we prevent or reverse these unhealthy habits in our children? There are some strategies that I have learnt from my colleague, Dr Paul Chadwick, a clinical psychologist who specialises in helping parents and children to change their unhealthy behaviours. Other strategies I have developed myself through my experiences in helping parents change their children's diets in the easiest way possible.

Chapter 15

Goals and rewards

Goals and rewards are very powerful tools to use to help children change their behaviour. If children beg for a sweet or toy and you say 'no' and they continue to plead for the item until you give in and buy it, they will quickly learn that begging and pleading pays off. Alternatively, if you always say 'no' and never give in, then your child will learn there is no point in even asking.

A better approach would be to use a goal-and-reward system whereby your child accumulates, for example, stars on a chart. When they have accumulated a pre-determined number of stars they get a pre-chosen reward, such as a new football kit, toy or day out. This encourages good behaviour and is extremely effective with children (and adults as well!).

Implementing a goal and reward system

Goals and rewards can go a long way in helping you to motivate your child, for example, to improve their eating behaviour or get them to be more physically active. Encouraging children to achieve their goals is a lot easier when there is a reward attached to it. It is very important that you give them realistic goals and do not set your children up for failure. Follow the guidelines below to achieve the best results when trying to motivate your children.

SMART goals

The SMART goal-setting system will help to break unhealthy eating and inactivity patterns and establish new healthier ones. Most of us set ourselves goals all the time, for example, to get work done, to do household chores. Mostly we are not aware that we are doing this. We also set goals in order to change major habits, for example, making New Year's resolutions to stop smoking or to exercise regularly. There are advantages to setting goals for your children. Goals are more likely to be achieved because they enhance a child's internal motivation – all kids like achieving goals – and can be a powerful way of reinforcing healthy behaviour. As the goal process is a joint effort, your children will feel that you are really interested in helping them and this will give them even more incentive to follow the rules. It is important to set goals that are mutually agreed and that work for both you and your children. The way to do this is to make sure that the goals you set are SMART.

So what is SMART?

SMART is an acronym and stands for:

S – Specific

M – Measurable

A – Achievable

R – Relevant

T – Time-limited

Specific

The goals you set need to be clearly defined and very specific. They shouldn't be ambiguous or easy to misinterpret. Which of these two scenarios is a good example of a specific goal?

a) Riding a bike to the shops; walking to school; reducing the number of chocolate bars eaten per week.
b) Doing more exercise; being healthier; eating less.

Answer: (a) is correct because these are all examples of a specific goal whereas the examples in (b) are too general and vague with no clear goal. 'Being healthier' is not specific and does not tell you anything about how you are going to *be* healthier.

Measurable

You must be able to measure whether your child has achieved the goal or not. Which of the following are good examples of measurable goals?

a) Riding my bike for 20 minutes twice a week; eating only two bags of crisps or two chocolate bars instead of seven a week.
b) Going for a bike ride; eating fewer crisps and chocolate bars a week.

Answer: (a) is correct because these examples can all be measured. 'Going for a bike ride' does not tell you how long you ride for or how often. 'Eating fewer crisps' does not tell you how many you will eat, whereas eating only two bags of crisps instead of seven a week is a very clearly defined and measurable goal.

Achievable

Are the goals realistic and possible to achieve? Be wary of being over-enthusiastic. Not achieving goals can seriously harm motivation and self-esteem. Which of the following are good examples of achievable goals?

a) Never eating crisps again; going to the gym five times a week.
b) Eating three chocolates rather than five a week; cycling three days a week for 20 minutes.

Answer: (b) is correct because these examples are achievable. How likely is it that a child will never eat a packet of crisps again? We cannot expect children to change their habits overnight and there is no point in pushing your children too hard. Change happens slowly over time.

Relevant

Is the goal relevant to what you are trying to achieve? Choose goals that will make a difference to the overall problem. Which of the examples below are good examples of relevant goals?

a) Choosing to cut down on crisps as they are high-fat and your child snacks on them daily.
b) Choosing not to eat doughnuts, which are high-GI and high in fat, but your child only eats them about three times a month.

Answer: (a) is correct because, as crisps are eaten regularly, reducing the amount of crisps your child eats will significantly reduce the number of high-fat snacks in their diet and make a significant contribution to improving their health, whereas reducing doughnuts, which they don't eat very often, will have very little impact on improving their health.

Time-limited

Make sure you set your children a time limit to achieve their goal. With the end in sight, it is easier to work harder to achieve it. Which of the following are good examples of time-limited goals?

a) Going swimming more often; walking to school more often.
b) Going swimming twice before next Tuesday; only eating pop tarts once in the next week.

Answer: (b) is correct as these examples all have a clearly defined time frame, whereas the examples in (a) do not tell you when the goal is to be achieved. By time-limiting goals, it makes them seem less overwhelming. Setting goals on a weekly time frame is an easier concept than the thought of practising a new behaviour for a longer period.

The golden rules of goal setting

Don't lose heart if your children fail to achieve their goals. Failure is an opportunity to learn. If they fail it usually means the goal was too difficult in the first place. Simply reduce the level of difficulty and try again the next week. For example, if they fail to walk to school four times a week instead of using the bus, then the following week set the goal of walking to school two times a week. Eventually, they will succeed and their confidence will be boosted. Remember, small, realistic, achievable goals are far better than big, unrealistic unachievable goals. Make sure that goals do not interfere with other family members. All family members must cooperate in order for your children to succeed.

Hard work deserves a reward

Children with low self-esteem are often unmotivated. Therefore, achieving goals and receiving rewards can give them a sense of achievement and raise their self-esteem and confidence. Rewards help promote desirable behaviour changes in children. If your children know that if they achieve their goal you will give them a reward, they are more likely to work harder to achieve it. Rewards really can help children to establish healthier eating practices and increase their level of physical activity.

Types of rewards

There are two types of reward: daily and goal-setting. Daily rewards are used to steer your child's behaviour in the right direction, while goal-setting rewards are used to help them achieve the overall result.

Daily rewards

Many of these types of rewards are ones you will already be providing on a daily basis. They are highly effective, simple, quick, cost nothing and can go a long way in improving your child's behaviour. Examples are praising your child, spontaneous displays of affection like giving them a quick hug or a kiss on the cheek, spending more time with them and giving them more attention. Another daily reward is avoiding negative talk. When talking about weight or eating, try not to lace your remarks with negative comments such as 'I try to help you, but you don't help yourself'. This can really damage a child's self-esteem and motivation. Try to replace such comments with positive thoughts such as 'You are doing so well', 'Tomorrow is another day', 'It will get easier'. For daily rewards to be effective, they should be given as close to the time of the desired behaviour as possible. For example, give praise as soon as you see your child doing something desirable. Don't save positive comments for later.

Goal-setting rewards

Goal-setting rewards should be negotiated with your child beforehand and used as a reward for achieving their SMART goals. Here are some dos and don'ts for setting rewards:

- Do make them meaningful to your children. Don't assume that what motivates you will motivate them.
- Do make sure effort and reward are matched. For example, don't use an expensive reward to motivate a small change in behaviour or vice versa.
- Do provide small frequent rewards rather than larger ones for the distant future. Remember, most of us desire instant gratification.
- Do make a record of their progress. Children often manage to pull the wool over their parents' eyes. Make sure you record their progress and accurately measure whether they achieve their goals or not.
- Don't set rewards that they might not be able to achieve. This will damage motivation and lead to mistrust.
- Don't use food as a reward. This reinforces the child's view that food is the only way to receive comfort or kind treatment during difficult times. Comfort eating is a major contributor to weight gain and one of the most difficult behaviours to change in overeating adults. It is best to curb it in childhood.

Examples of goal-setting rewards

After achieving the goal, for example, of attending two

swimming sessions per week, why not take your child shopping with a small set budget for them to spend?

Or let them spend the school dinner money or bus money they save after taking a packed lunch to school four out of five days for two months, or walking to school four times a week. The saved money can then be used to buy any non-food reward.

Here are some other examples of rewards:

- Theatre trip
- Magazine
- Cinema ticket
- Video/DVD
- Art and craft equipment
- Clothes, hair accessories
- New bag or stationery for school

Goal and reward chart

Charts are a good visual way to monitor your children's goals and rewards. Once a goal and suitable reward have been agreed, they can be written on the chart, which can then be checked daily to monitor how your children are progressing. Once a week on an agreed day, the chart can be tallied to see whether the goal has been achieved. For example, if the goal was to walk to school four times per week and the chart is marked with, say, a tick every time your children walk to school then, if there are four ticks on the chart they can receive their pre-agreed reward. The marks can be ticks, stars or smiley faces for achieving goals – or whatever you like. The chart can

Example of a goal and reward chart

Goal: To have no more than one packet of crisps per day for five days of the week.

	Mon	Tues	Wed	Thurs	Fri	Sat	Sun
Achieved	☺	☺		☺	☺		☺

Reward: Family trip to the park

be used to motivate your children to change almost any type of unhealthy behaviour. There are many types of goal and reward charts, which you and your children can make together. See above for a simple example.

Goal and reward chart guidelines

- Never withhold a reward as a punishment.
- If children fail to achieve their goal, avoid making them feel like a failure. Always congratulate them for having a go and suggest setting an easier goal, or ask if there is anything the family can do to help.
- Do not discuss their failure to achieve their goal when you are angry or upset with them.
- Never use their failure as a way to emphasise negative aspects of their personality. If a child behaves badly, criticise the action – not their character.

Case study – goals and rewards

Tammy was nine years old, weighed 45kg and was 130cm tall, giving her a BMI of 27 (obese category). Her mum had tried everything to help her lose weight. Not only was she concerned about her young daughter's health, but she knew that Tammy was constantly being teased by boys in her class, and this was affecting her school work. Tammy was very aware that she was overweight. Her mum felt she had an insatiable appetite for food, which she could not change. Not only did Tammy enjoy three hot meals daily – usually involving two helpings – she also had a sweet tooth, and often spent all her pocket money on sweets. Her mother tried changing Tammy's meals to healthier ones but her daughter refused to eat them and would run out of the kitchen. Later she would be found snacking secretly on junk food.

Tammy's mother tried daily walks to the park and preparing low-fat home-cooked family meals, but nothing seemed to help. Tammy always found a way to break her diet and load up on crisps, cakes and chocolate.

Her mother needed to find a way to motivate Tammy to make the changes without forcing her to do it. After struggling with the problem for two years, her mother attended a lecture I was giving on 'How to motivate your child to eat healthier food'. This explained different techniques used by nutritionists and behavioural experts to initiate healthy lifestyle and dietary changes, such as the goal-and-reward system. Tammy's mother sensed that this might work for Tammy. I met Tammy and her mum for a consultation. Tammy loved presents and surprises and her mum thought that if they could make losing weight fun for Tammy she might be more inclined to stick to it.

Her mother purchased a large-poster-sized piece of cardboard and asked her daughter to help design it – which she happily began doing using her favourite markers and pens. They then sat down and decided that every Sunday they would discuss the goals and reward for that week. Her mother also set goals for herself and they made a pact to help each other achieve them. This was the first time that Tammy appeared excited about the idea of losing weight. Her first week's goal was to drink four glasses of water a day and to replace her usual intake of fruit juices and sugary soft drinks with sugar-free drinks. As a reward, her mother would take her and two friends to a theme park, a treat usually saved up for birthdays. Tammy was so excited. She called her friends and told them what had been promised. Including her friends in the reward programme was an excellent idea as they helped make sure Tammy was not tempted to break the rules at school or on the way home.

Tammy stuck to the first week's goal and the girls got to spend the day at the theme park. Part of the deal was that the girls could not spend their money on sweets and unhealthy snacks. The following week, Tammy set herself a goal not to eat chocolates. Again she succeeded and was rewarded with a mid-week movie. Her mother chose the same goal and they worked as a team, avoiding the chocolate aisles at their local supermarket and buying healthy sugar-free chocolate-flavoured desserts. It was not all plain sailing, though. One week Tammy set herself a goal not to snack between meals. This was a bad idea, as children should eat a couple of snacks through the day to keep their sugar levels balanced and avoid falling into the hunger trap. Tammy experienced her first failure and felt really bad about it. I suggested to her mother that she advise Tammy to reset the goal to eat only healthy low-GI foods as snacks and to include up to three snacks a day. Tammy agreed to try and enjoyed experimenting with different fruits and frozen yoghurt treats, which satisfied her sweet tooth. Gradually, Tammy began eating a healthy, balanced nutritional diet and her weight began to drop. After six months of goal-setting and reward-giving, she had lost 3kg and now maintains her weight while she grows taller. However, her greatest achievement has been to break her constant sweet tooth cravings by learning to enjoy eating a variety of low-GI carbohydrates, which help to balance her sugar levels. Now, although she no longer craves sweets and biscuits, she still enjoys occasional sweet treats without becoming addicted to them.

Even though Tammy and her family have got on top of her previous eating problems, the family continues to use the goal-and-reward system to initiate different changes, such as helping her father give up smoking. For every week that he did not smoke he got a new reward. For example, the family might stay quiet and let him sleep late on Saturday mornings, or cook him breakfast in bed. Tammy's brother used the method to help motivate him to study for his exams, and Tammy still uses it to motivate her to stick to healthy foods. Most children find it hard to give up something they love, such as sweets, especially if they have nothing to replace it with. But by setting goals and negotiating suitable rewards you can get children to change their unhealthy eating habits.

Should I punish my child?

Driven to the point of no return? Feel like punishing your child? For many of us, growing up with regular bouts of punishments was the 'norm' as these were meant to deter us from behaving badly and repeating our terrible acts. But how often were we unfairly punished just because our parents were in a bad mood or couldn't explain clearly what they expected from us. Today, parents are fortunate to have access to many new techniques that explain clearly how to encourage the right behaviour from their children without the need for punishment.

Punishing your children should be a last resort and, to really be effective, a rare occurrence. If all attempts at improving your children's behaviour using goals and rewards fails, or if a child's behaviour is serious – hitting, swearing or stealing, for example – then punishment may be necessary in the short term. However, regular punishment is a dangerous path to follow, as it is likely to create a huge gap between you and your children, causing them to see you as the enemy and to dislike everything you represent. This can cause even more problems through withdrawal of cooperation, feelings of guilt, blame and animosity on both sides, which often leads to problem behaviour such as binge eating. Remember, punishment may temporarily stop bad behaviour but it never helps in starting good behaviour.

Chapter 16

Children need role models

It is important to become a good role model for your children. Simply telling your children to do one thing while you do another thing is bad parenting. Do you find yourself sitting on the sofa in front of the television scoffing a packet of crisps while you tell your children to go outside and play football? If so, you are going to teach your children one thing – that you are a hypocrite! Parents have told me that they have tried everything to get their children to eat fruit and vegetables, but the child refuses. More often than not, if I ask the parent, 'What fruit and vegetables do you eat regularly?' the common response is 'Oh, I don't really like fruit and vegetables!' Children learn by example and will usually only eat what their role models eat, be they parents, peers, sports stars, pop stars or television personalities.

It really upsets me to see children's idols promoting crisps, sugary soft-drinks and fast food in adverts. It's no wonder children today are addicted to eating these foods, they are simply copying their role models. Educate your children that stars get paid a lot of money to advertise these foods. They don't actually eat or drink these foods regularly themselves or they wouldn't be as slim or fit as they are! Please support any efforts made to stop advertising unhealthy foods to children on television. This will make a parent's job a lot more effective.

Case study – role model

Every day Martin would come home from school, tummy rumbling and ready for lunch. Martin's mum worked half days and so was always home ready with food on the table. They would always eat their meals together. Their favourites were fried fish and chips, sausages and mash, beef stew and rice, or beef sandwiches. Then they would have a dessert – ice cream, jelly and custard or bread and butter pudding – to finish off. Later they would watch the daily soaps and children's programmes, while managing to polish off a packet of biscuits, two packets of crisps and half a litre of flavoured milk or fruit juice with added sugar. When Martin's dad came home in the evening, the family would eat a main meal consisting of home-made roast, or a stew, or a pasta dish. Twice a week, they would eat out at their local Indian or Chinese restaurant.

Martin's mother began to notice that he was larger than other nine-year-old boys and that he was developing a protuding stomach. She began to wonder if he was slightly overweight. She had struggled with her own weight all her life, but having tried hundreds of diets, had given up and accepted her size 16 frame. She told me that she had a beautiful son and a husband that loved her, therefore being overweight was no longer important.

However, when Martin began to complain of being out of breath while running around the playground and complained that kids were calling him 'fatty pants', she knew she had to intervene for his sake. She decided to put him on a diet and tried to get him to do exercise by buying him a soccer ball. She also began making special meals from recipes in her old diet books – and told him that he should kick the soccer ball around while she watched television.

Martin began to rebel and refused to eat his mother's 'diet' lunches. Instead, he bought junk food on his way home. He also refused to play with the ball she had bought him. In the evenings, his mother would prepare Martin his special 'diet' meal, while she and her husband ate their normal meals. She cut out their twice-weekly visits to the Indian and Chinese restaurants and ordered takeaways for herself and her husband while Martin was served a pre-prepared 'healthy range' meal from her local supermarket. She also enrolled Martin in a martial arts class, but he refused to go, saying he did not want to miss his afternoon television programmes.

When Martin came to visit me, he was resentful and angry, saying that his mum was being very mean and he could not understand why she was punishing him. I took his blood pressure, and checked his weight, height and waist circumference. I calculated that Martin was obese and his waist circumference put him in the high-risk category. He had accumulated most of his weight around his stomach and this was a cause for concern and immediate action. I began by explaining to him that his mother was trying to help by trying to improve his health and fitness. However, he refused to listen, saying it was unfair that his mum still got to watch afternoon television and eat whatever she wanted and he didn't. He also told me that his mum loved his father more because she got him takeaways and refused to buy them for Martin. I was immediately aware that his parents needed guidance on how to be effective role models. Most children at this age are more inclined to imitate their parents' actions than do what they say. The family needed to develop a healthier lifestyle that would suit all of them.

I began by instructing Martin's parents on the importance of setting a healthy example. I asked his mother if there was anything other than watching television she would like to do in the afternoons. She said she would like to go back to the aqua-aerobic classes held at her local health club. She also admitted that she would like to lose 12kg – although she still assured me it was not that important to her. His father said he would like to get back into cycling. He had been an ardent cyclist in his youth and always felt a pull to take it up again. I suggested that Martin attend his martial arts classes on the same days that his mother went to aqua-aerobic classes and that on other days they walk to the park or to a local playground where Martin could run around and play. I also recommended that his father take Martin for bicycle rides in the early evenings and at weekends. I then suggested that his mother reserved television for later on in the evening and recorded their favourite programmes. I also recommended that they try to do something active with Martin every weekend, such as kicking the ball around, taking long walks in their favourite park, or going for family bicycle rides.

It was imperative that the family began eating the same food. I assured them that there were simple changes that they could make to convert their meals into low-fat, low-GI, healthier fare. Instead of fried fish, they could have grilled or baked fish with steamed vegetables or baked butternut. Instead of fatty beef stews, they could have chicken breast stews with basmati or brown rice. Roast meals could still be eaten but with a low-fat gravy and baked (not roasted) new potatoes, mixed salad or steamed vegetables such as Brussels sprouts. I told them it was important that Martin saw them all eating the same food and was not informed that it was special healthy food. Rather, he should see them as normal family meals. As for eating out, I suggested they continue with the tradition but only once a week, and to avoid fried food or white rice, or dishes served with heavy cream or oil. I suggested that they save the other family outing for movies or evening strolls.

I asked them to bring Martin back in a month for a follow-up consultation. When I saw them again, Martin seemed much happier and relaxed. He was wearing his karate outfit, which his mother said he would not take off, and had asked to go to classes twice a week. She said it had been fairly simple to make the recommended meal changes and Martin had barely noticed that the meals were healthier. The family still ate out, but they never ordered the Chinese fried foods or white rice and always had a spicy soup to start, followed by a stir-fry with extra vegetables in oyster sauce. In Indian restaurants they ordered from the Tandoori section of the menu, avoiding the rice and oily high-GI breads. Martin's weight was down as was his mother's. Her husband said she was far happier now and seemed more confident.

Chapter 17

Triggers

A trigger is something that sets off certain behaviours. For example, walking past the newsagent may trigger the urge to buy sweets or crisps. Walking past the pub may trigger the urge for a drink. One trigger may then trigger something else. Having a pint of beer may trigger the urge for a cigarette, for example. So you may decide to avoid the pub to help you give up smoking. It is important to try to reduce daily triggers that cause us either to do something unhealthy or avoid doing something healthy.

External triggers

There are two types of trigger, the first is external. Grabbing a snack every time you walk past the fridge is an example of an external trigger – the fridge being the trigger. The second type is internal triggers, which are thoughts or feelings that cause you to behave in a certain way. I will discuss internal triggers later on. In order to help your children become healthier, you will need to become aware of triggers that cause them to overeat, or remain inactive, and try to prevent these, while boosting the triggers that cause them to adopt healthy behaviour. Certain things in your children's environments, either at home or at school, may trigger unhealthy behaviour. For example, the desire to eat chocolate when seeing an open packet lying on the table, or watching television all day because they are copying their older brother. In order to prevent unhealthy behaviour you need to work out how you can replace these unhelpful triggers with new healthy ones.

Activity Triggers:	Inactivity Triggers:
Playing outdoors.	Television.
Having fun active things to play with such as soccer balls, skipping rope.	Playstation, computer games, Internet.
Routine walks, such as walking to school.	Sedentary parents or other family members.
Limiting time spent on computer and television.	Not having anything planned/ boredom.
Joining a sports club, enrolling in a dance or swimming club.	Lack of opportunities to be active outdoors, such as bad weather, safety fears.
Having someone to be active with.	No one to play outside with.
Structure and routine.	Presence of other inactive people; having nothing active planned.
Nutritious food that gives children more energy to be active.	Embarrassment over size.

Examples of healthy eating triggers:	**Examples of unhealthy eating triggers:**
Presence of healthy foods – a fruit bowl on the table, chopped fruit in the fridge left at eye-level.	Availability of chocolate, crisps and other unhealthy foods in the home.
Pictures of healthy food on the fridge or kitchen cupboard.	Watching cookery programmes on TV.
Eating together as a family at the table.	Being left alone to eat in front of the television.
Seeing family and friends eating healthy foods and being active.	Seeing other people eating unhealthy foods and being sedentary.
No access to unhealthy foods at home.	School dinners, peer pressure. Spare pocket money or money to spend on sweets.
Shopping with children after a meal, i.e. on full stomachs.	Not having healthy alternatives around.
Ready made healthy snacks at home.	Long breaks between meals.
Goals and rewards.	Special occasions and eating out.
Knowledge about the food we eat.	Unstructured days – not planning meals.
Complimenting children.	Making negative comments.

Dealing with unhealthy eating triggers

Here are some examples of triggers that encourage unhealthy eating along with suggestions of ways to deal with them:

Trigger: Access to unhealthy food at home.

Ways to deal with it:

- Don't buy high-GI snack foods.
- Place treats somewhere that is not visible to the child – a locked kitchen cupboard will do!
- Never leave unhealthy food lying around, such as crisps or biscuits.

Trigger: Having money to spend at break time.

Ways to deal with it:

- Offer your children an incentive or reward to give up their school dinners and take healthy packed lunches to school.
- Limit the amount of money available to your children to spend on sweets. Give them exactly the right amount of money for what they need.
- Use a goal and reward chart. The goal is to save money by not buying school dinners or snack foods at school. The reward – in two weeks they will be able to afford a new toy, game, book or something else they really want.

Healthy eating triggers

Here are some examples of triggers that promote healthy eating behaviour:

Trigger: Making healthy foods easily available.

- Make sure there is always a fruit bowl where your children can see it that is within easy reach.
- Fill the kitchen with healthy low-GI snacks.
- Cook healthy meals together.
- Plan in advance for meals and days out.
- Prepare healthy and filling lunch boxes.

Here are some examples of visual triggers that promote healthy eating:

- Place pictures of healthy, delicious-looking food on the fridge door.
- Make sure they watch films and read articles and activity books with healthy food messages.
- Create visually stimulating plates of food. Be inventive with vegetables, use different colours and shapes to make them look enticing.
- Be a role model – make sure your children see you eating healthy foods.

Physical activity triggers

Here are some examples of triggers that promote physical activity outdoors:

- Play in the garden with your children.
- Play a weekly game of soccer, organise egg-and-spoon races, buy a hula hoop and skipping rope, try juggling, play bat and ball against the wall – begin to initiate games and hope they will follow.

- Take a Frisbee or ball to the park.
- Go rollerblading or roller-skating in the park.
- Organise family walks or cycling trips.

Here are some examples of triggers that promote physical activity indoors:

- Give them housework to do.
- Turn up the music and start dancing with them – most younger kids will love this.
- Get them to help you cook low-GI meals.
- Leave skipping ropes, hula hoops, Twister lying around.
- Stick up posters and other visual reminders to stimulate activity – such as pin-up pictures of your child's favourite sport or sporting hero.

It is much easier to encourage your children to increase doing something that they already do to a limited extent. For example, if they play football or go to dance class once a week, then try to increase it to twice a week. If they enjoy walking the dog and usually do it after school, then try to get them to walk the dog in the mornings before school, or – even better – walk them and the dog to school and you get fit too!

Dealing with inactivity triggers

Television, the Internet and computer games can all trigger inactivity. Here's how to deal with them:

- Have set times for watching television, such as after the evening meal.

- Lock the remote control away, or remove the batteries. This means they have to get up every time they want to change the channel.
- Use a stopwatch and, every time the television is turned on, start the countdown. After one to two hours, switch off the television.
- Have planned activities or projects to do at night.
- Turn on the television only to watch favourite shows. Play music or games at other times.
- Offer a reward, such as 10p for every minute under the agreed maximum time spent watching television.

Sedentary parents can be a trigger for children to be sedentary themselves. Here are some suggestions to overcome this:

- Join a local sports centre together – get involved with children's swimming clubs.
- Train for a charity event together, such as a sponsored walk or mini-marathon.
- Take up a new family sport.
- Play an active family game after dinner instead of watching television together.
- Ask your children to be your personal trainer.

Case study – external triggers

Tim was a headstrong boy and hated being told what to do. He often got into trouble at school for failing to follow his teacher's instructions and disturbing his classmates. He found it hard to sit still for more than a couple of minutes at a time and constantly fidgeted. After being given detention and extra homework once too often, he was sent to the school nurse. He was then referred to a paediatrician, who diagnosed a mild case of attention deficit hyperactivity disorder (ADHD). Tim's case was not serious enough to require medication but his parents were given a list of other ways to help calm him down.

They were told that he should avoid eating stimulating foods such as sugary sweets and fizzy drinks containing caffeine, as they could be contributing to his restlessness and his inability to concentrate. Changing their son's dietary habits was tough for the family as they had very little knowledge about food and nutrition. Both parents had full-time jobs and mostly ate ready-made meals, snacked on biscuits and chocolate and drank caffeinated beverages such as coffee and cola soft drinks to get them through the day. Their son lived on a similar diet. The paediatrician convinced Tim's parents that, if they made certain lifestyle changes, their son's condition could improve dramatically. The paediatrician arranged for them to see me for advice.

Initially, I recommended that they begin modifying Tim's diet by adding low-GI carbohydrate foods such as sourdough bread, fruit and yoghurt to reduce his sugar cravings. His mother confided in me that it was almost impossible to get Tim to do anything he did not want to do, let alone listen to direct instructions. I helped them come up with a strategy that would motivate Tim to follow a healthier diet.

The plan involved leaving subtle triggers lying around the house and implanting healthy ideas into Tim's mind. His mother began by changing her shopping habits, replacing unhealthy snack food with healthier versions, such as nut and raisin mixes, sugar-free cordials and wholemeal pitta bread sandwiches. She also decided to devote more time to baking and cooking, a pastime she had enjoyed before she had children. She cooked at the weekends, doubling up the quantities and separating them into portions that were frozen to be eaten later on in the week. Then she set about leaving visible triggers around the house. She filled up three transparent containers with dried fruit and nuts, oat biscuits and an assortment of sugar-free sweets and chewing gum, which she placed on top of the kitchen counter. She also made sure there was always a bowl on the kitchen table filled with fruit for Tim to snack on.

When Tim began noticing the changes, his mother explained that she had a sudden urge to do more cooking and eat more fruit and vegetables. His father said he wanted to learn how to cook. He started making a 'special omelette delight' on wholegrain toast on Saturday mornings. After seeing his dad in the kitchen, Tim surprised his parents by asking if he could learn how to cook too. He began helping his mother prepare simple healthy meals in the evenings – his expertise lay in throwing a piece of pasta against the wall to see if it was cooked! It was impossible for the family to eat home–made meals every day but when they did eat out or were forced to eat prepared meals, Tim's mother always checked the labels and bought low-GI meals.

Tim's parents also cut out pictures of healthy food and posted them on the refrigerator. In the afternoons, whenever one of them called to check on Tim, they would mention how tasty their apple had been or how awful they felt after eating a bar of chocolate. Another clever trigger was devised to get Tim to drink more water. His mother bought a large transparent water canister and every day she placed a different type of fruit in the water – Tim's favourite was strawberry slices. She also filled different-coloured juice bottles with ready-made sugar-free cordial mixtures and put them in the fridge. She stopped buying colas containing caffeine and sugar.

The next step was to trigger Tim into using up his excess energy in healthy, active ways. His parents did not like him to be outdoors on his own when they weren't around to watch him and he had difficulty making friends. So they bought a cheap exercise bicycle, which they both began to use in front of him. Tim's father also bought a boxing set, which he set up in the living room. This turned out to be an excellent release for Tim's aggression and he asked his parents if he could go to boxing classes. The exercise bike proved to be a success with the whole family. Their fitness levels improved and they began planning weekend cycling trips. Tim loved this as his parents gave him the title of 'captain', and it was his job to co-ordinate their routes – with a bit of help from his father.

Tim's behaviour gradually began to improve and he did not seem so restless and agitated. His studies improved, too, and he was no longer thrown out of class for disruptive behaviour. Tim had previously found it hard to get to sleep and his parents often let him stay up late watching videos. Once he started boxing classes and changed his eating habits, however, his sleep pattern was much improved.

His mum and dad hardly ever mentioned health, diet or exercise, and only spoke about the changes in terms of enjoyment and fun. The family as a whole benefited from the changes, and his parents now enjoy the time spent with their son.

Internal triggers

It is really helpful to be aware of internal triggers that can cause children to overeat and remain inactive. There are four main types – hunger, cravings, unhelpful thoughts and negative feelings. These internal triggers need to be understood and addressed if children are to adopt a healthier attitude towards food and exercise. Internal triggers can be more complex than external triggers. Internal and external triggers often interact to produce a particular pattern of unhealthy behaviour.

How do we deal with internal triggers?

Many of the strategies that parents use to deal with external triggers can be used to deal with internal ones. It is also really helpful to deal with your own internal struggles with food or physical activity because children will observe and copy your behaviour. If your children observe you turning to food for comfort in times of stress, then so will they. Bad habits are hard to break, so the sooner you can begin to implement healthy coping strategies for yourself and your children, the easier it will be to stick to a healthier lifestyle.

I will briefly discuss each of the four principal internal triggers and offer some simple strategies to deal with them. It is highly recommended that you also try them for yourself if you are to be an effective role model. Remember, it is not acceptable to behave in one way and expect your children to behave in a different way; actions definitely speak louder than words.

Hunger

Hunger is a physiological need. It is our body's way of letting us know that it requires feeding and is stimulated by a drop in blood-sugar levels. If hunger is poorly managed it often leads to overeating and irregular food patterns, which are a major cause of overweight. When we are genuinely hungry it is harder to make wise food choices as we are willing to eat anything in sight just to stop that gnawing feeling in our stomachs. In this situation it is far too easy to reach for a quick fix, such as chocolate biscuits or a packet of crisps. For example, you have been at work all day or out shopping and you arrive home feeling ravenous. You begin to make the family meal but you just cannot ignore the groaning hunger in the pit of your stomach. Before you know it, you are snacking and by the time you sit down to eat your meal, you have already had the equivalent of a meal made up of unhealthy foods. Many children have lunch between 12pm and 1.30pm and have to wait until 6pm or 7pm for their parents to return from work and prepare dinner. This means they will be home alone unattended for several hours. They start to get hungry in the late afternoon and begin to snack on sugary snacks. At other times we start eating snacks simply because everyone else in the office is, or we are just bored. So be aware of why you eat and whether you or your children are eating out of habit or are generally hungry.

The problem: Your children eat a packet of biscuits when they come home from school or eat lots of junk food after swimming practice.

Suggestions:

- Make sure your children eat meals at set meal times and have up to three healthy snacks per day.
- Prepare healthy, low-GI snacks that are waiting for your children as soon as they come home from school. For example have a sandwich or pieces of fruit ready, or bring a piece of fruit and yoghurt with you when you collect your children from swimming.

Cravings

Cravings are what drive most of us to eat between meals. A craving is the desire to eat something even when we are not hungry. There are three main differences between hunger and cravings:

- When we feel hungry we will eat whatever will fill us up but we get a craving for a particular food, such as a chocolate bar – and only that will do.
- Cravings disappear after 20 minutes but hunger gets worse.
- Cravings generally reflect a psychological desire rather than a physiological one. For example, if you ignore hunger signals for long enough it will affect your energy levels and

you will feel weak and tired. However, there are no harmful effects from ignoring a craving.

The problem: Your children get a sudden urge for a big bar of chocolate or bowl of ice cream even though they are not hungry.

Suggestions:

- Ride it out; cravings only last for about 20 minutes and then disappear.
- Distraction; get your child to do something mentally involving for 20 minutes – such as reading a book, doing a puzzle, physical exercise, phoning a friend, or doing homework.
- Damage limitation: don't have high-GI, fatty snacks in the house – if they are there it will be difficult to control the craving.
- Indulge the craving in a small way. If the craving is for a healthy or medium GI food, then don't bother restricting it.

Unhelpful thoughts

Our thoughts affect the way we behave and whether we change our ways or not. Thoughts can be divided into two groups:

- Helpful thoughts enable you and your children to stick to your new healthier habits and lifestyle changes.
- Unhelpful thoughts make it difficult for you and your children to keep to your new healthier habits and lifestyle changes. For example, if your children believe that everyone will laugh at them in PE, they will try to avoid it by pretending to be unwell.

It is therefore important that you and your children build

positive thoughts about eating and being active and abandon negative or unhelpful thoughts.

The problem: Thoughts such as – 'No one likes me because I am fat.' 'Everyone will laugh at me if I try this.' 'It's not fair that I can't eat the same things as my friends.'

Suggestions:

- Explain to your children that if people don't like them because they are overweight then they are not very nice people and your children shouldn't want them as a friend. Instead, find friends who will like them for who they are.
- Make lists of positive thoughts and read them regularly.
- Talk the thoughts through with your children and teach them how to turn negative thoughts into positive ones. Write down positive thoughts and stick them on your children's bedroom wall.

Negative feelings

Feelings can lead to overeating in a number of different ways. Here are a few examples:

- Boredom: This is perhaps the greatest contributor to overeating. Children will always want to eat when they have nothing to do – eating is a very enjoyable activity!
- Celebrations and rewards: We celebrate happy occasions such as birthdays and Christmas by eating. Food is often given to reward good behaviour or for a special achievement.
- Unhappiness and stress: Food is often used to calm the nerves or to relieve feelings of sadness. This can lead to excess weight gain.

Here are some examples of feelings and thoughts that lead to healthy and unhealthy behaviours.

- **Negative feelings that lead to unhealthy behaviours:** boredom, sadness, loneliness, depression, anger, stress, anxiety.
- **Unhelpful thoughts that lead to unhealthy behaviours:** I'll start tomorrow, It doesn't really matter, I need or deserve a treat.
- **Positive feelings that lead to healthy behaviours:** happiness, confidence, excitement, being positive, being motivated, enthusiasm, being calm and relaxed.
- **Helpful thoughts that lead to healthy behaviours:** I know I'll feel bad if I give in to my craving for a chocolate bar. I would rather get my reward than have a second helping.

The problem: Feelings of boredom, unhappiness and stress.

Suggestions:

- Understand the thoughts behind the feelings and find a way to tackle those. For example, if your children feel sad it might result from thinking that no one likes them. Once you know this you can help your children to understand that this is not correct and that there are people who do like them for who they are.
- Make time to listen and talk to your children so they have the opportunity to tell you what they are struggling with.
- Use distraction – find a non-eating way of taking their mind off the bad feeling. Eventually they will not need food to cope with such feelings.

Part Five

Putting It All Together

Chapter 18
The future

If your children are overweight the best gift you can give them is the gift of love and good health. The consequences of obesity are very serious. The chances are very likely that if it is not addressed early on, your children will probably grow into obese adolescents and then adults, at risk of many serious medical conditions. The prospect of overcoming obesity is severely handicapped if it is not tackled in childhood. As one gets older it becomes much harder to lose excess weight and keep it off. Once you are overweight or obese, you will always have the tendency to gain weight. Therefore, the advice in this book, if implemented correctly early on, can prevent wasted years of misery and suffering.

As a parent, you obviously want the best for your children. Yet it can also be very frustrating when you are aware that your children's behaviours are bad for their health. You have the knowledge to correct them but your children just won't listen or cooperate with you. However, by now you should be aware that talking is often not the best way to implement change in your children's eating or activity patterns. It is far more beneficial to show them what to do by making changes to the whole family's diet so your children don't feel they are being picked on but are being included in the whole family's efforts to get healthier. Always take into account the emotional strain of being an overweight or obese child. If your children are very sensitive about their weight, don't make it a focal point – trust me they are very aware already. Instead of singling out the fact that they need to lose weight, talk about the whole family's need to improve their health. Remember, this programme will benefit your whole family. It is possible that every family member can become overweight at some point in the future, so getting healthy is in everyone's best interest.

How do I put all my new knowledge into practice?

Now that you have the tools needed to transform your kid into a superkid it is important that you start to put your new knowledge into practice. Changing eating and activity habits and routines can be a slow process but worth the effort in the long run. There will be setbacks – remember, none of us is perfect and perfection is not what we are striving for but rather making small changes over a long period of time. An important reason why diets don't work is that they require so many large changes to be made in a short space of time. Once your motivation levels drop, this means a return to previous habits. The difference with my approach is that small, gradual changes are achievable for the whole family. Nobody should feel that they are on a diet or feel hungry at any point – in fact, quite the opposite. You should feel full most of the time. Use the goal-and-reward system to implement small but relevant changes to your children's lifestyle – both in the foods they eat and in the levels of physical activity they do.

Never give up

If things don't go the way you expect or want them to go, don't give up. Reassess the situation and change your game plan. Realising that your children may already have low self-esteem and may even feel failures, will encourage you to set small, realistic goals that they can achieve and which will boost their confidence. Then you can set further achievable goals, allowing them to build their confidence and get healthier at the same time. It can be very tempting to set ambitious targets when you and your children are feeling highly motivated, but in a short while that motivation might dwindle, yet you still need to make sure that the goals will be achieved. If they are not being achieved, then reset them at a slightly lower level and try again. Never give up!

Work as a family

Remember you need to work together as a family to achieve the aim of transforming your family's health and this experience can only help to bring you all much closer together. Don't underestimate how important a role model you are to your children.

Accept this opportunity to improve your own health too and relive your fun childhood memories by playing games and doing physical activities that you used to love doing as a child. Experimenting with new foods and recipes can be exciting and working as a team will teach your kids the skills that they will need to shop and cook for themselves when they leave the nest. Children naturally love anything creative and cooking is very creative and imaginative. Try creating your own low-GI recipes and experimenting with all the ideas and suggestions I have given you.

Begin improving your family's health now!

This book contains a lot of information on improving nutrition and increasing physical activity levels. It would truly take a superfamily to implement all these changes immediately. What is more realistic and achievable is to start gradually and make small realistic changes. As all families are different, it is now up to you to decide, using the information in the other chapters, how you are going to improve your family's health.

For children who never eat breakfast, starting to eat a morning meal daily would be a great improvement. For other children, reducing the amount of sugary drinks they consume would be a great boost to their health. It is important to make any changes as a family. So get your family together and explain some of the principles you have learnt from this book. Then you can decide as a family which changes you would like to make and which are realistic and achievable. Using the SMART guidelines and the goal and reward chart, I recommend you start with

one healthy eating goal and one physical activity goal per week. Make sure this is achieved and always keep your end of the deal by giving the agreed reward. Make the goal and reward chart with your children and decide which goals would significantly improve their health. There is no point setting a goal to, for example, give up chocolates during the week if your children prefer crisps and sweets. The goal needs to be relevant to your family and lifestyle. I wish you lots of success.

Seeking professional help

There are various places to seek professional help if you are concerned about the health of your child. A useful starting point is the NHS Direct information service. NHS Direct operates a 24-hour service, providing confidential information on:

- What to do if you or your family are feeling ill.
- Particular health conditions.
- Local healthcare services, such as doctors, dentists or late-night-opening pharmacies.
- Self-help and support organisations.

If you are concerned about your children's health, growth or weight then make an appointment to see your GP, who will be able to diagnose if there is a problem or not. Your GP may decide to refer your children to a specialist. If your children are obese, they may be referred to a paediatrician to make sure there is not a medical cause behind their obesity. A few hospitals in the UK provide a specialist paediatric obesity clinic, which deals specifically with child obesity and its associated problems. These clinics are often multidisciplinary (more than one health professional works there) and they may include a doctor, nurse, dietitian, psychologist and physiotherapist. They may also have an exercise referral scheme or other plan to help your children become more physically active.

These specialist clinics deal mainly with children who have developed medical problems owing to their weight, such as sleep apnoea (difficulties breathing at night during sleep), diabetes or asthma. Another useful option is to seek the advice of a dietitian who is skilled in dealing with overweight children and uses behavioural techniques, rather than calorie restriction. You can be referred by your GP or paediatrician to see an NHS dietitian or contact one privately. See www.bda.uk.com for further information. If you require support in dealing with your children's or your own weight problem then contact TOAST (The Obesity Awareness and Solutions Trust) for specialised help and support. If your children are otherwise well and you would prefer a more holistic option that does not involve seeing a doctor or visiting a hospital then the MEND Programme may be suitable.

The MEND Programme

MEND is a proven multidisciplinary prevention and treatment programme for overweight and obese children and their families. MEND has been developed over a period of five years by me and my colleague, Dr Paul Chadwick (BSc MA DClin Psy), a clinical psychologist and recognised expert in the field of childhood obesity. We designed the programme because we felt that the majority of overweight and obese families had nowhere to turn for suitable and effective treatment.

MEND conducted a highly successful pilot study between September 2002 and March 2003, which has been peer-reviewed and published in *The Journal of Human Nutrition and Dietetics* (Feb 2005). Both the curriculum and the underlying research are supported by the Department of Health and the Institute of Child Health. The pilot showed statistically significant results in important measurements such as waist circumference, cardiovascular fitness and self-esteem.

How does the MEND Programme work?

The key to MEND's success is its integrated approach, combining all the elements the medical community knows to be vital in preventing and treating obesity: family involvement, increasing physical activity and reducing inactivity, dietary education and behavioural modification. MEND stands for: a healthy Mind, sufficient Exercise, good Nutrition and a balanced Diet. Families who take part in MEND are given access to tried and tested information and skills in all four of these areas. This provides them with a foundation for feeling healthier, fitter and generally happier – *for the rest of their lives*.

The MEND Programme comprises 18 two-hour sessions. It is currently aimed at 7–12 year-old children. Each child should be accompanied by at least one parent at each session. This is because the programme is as much about educating parents in how they can support their children as it is about teaching the children themselves.

MEND was conceived as a community-based programme. It must be stressed that MEND is *not* a diet and does not emphasise rapid weight loss, as this can be dangerous for growing children. Unlike diets, which do not typically deliver lasting results, MEND provides a responsible, reliable and effective foundation for healthy living – for life. Of course, by following the MEND principles, you can lose weight naturally and in a healthy manner.

Each two-hour session comprises one hour of fun and practical learning, focusing either on mind or nutrition/diet aspects, and one hour of exercise. While the majority of the learning sessions are attended by children and parents together, there are some that are intended for parents alone – particularly mind sessions dealing with behavioural modelling.

In brief, the programme consists of:

- **Mind** – eight sessions to improve self-esteem, increase understanding of behavioural modelling and to help families overcome difficulties in interacting with food and each other, using tools such as goal-and-reward setting, stimulus control and internal and external triggers.
- **Exercise** – 18 sessions of fun activities and group play on land and in water to build up strength and fitness. The exercises are geared to the fitness levels and physical abilities of overweight and obese children. They are graded and structured and involve group play so that everyone can join in and nobody feels left out.

- **Nutrition and Diet** – eight sessions focusing on simple and practical healthy-eating techniques (such as low-fat, low-sugar, low-salt, portion control, five fruits a day), combined with cutting-edge scientific advice on reducing foods with a high GI. The focus on practical education encourages you to trial and sample special low-GI MEND recipes. It also includes a supermarket tour, which educates children about nutritional labelling and allows them to apply their new-found knowledge in everyday life.

Benefits of MEND

For overweight or obese children:

- Fun!
- Increased education building a foundation for healthy living.
- Improved fitness and body composition.
- Increased self-confidence, and self-esteem, and reduced bullying.
- Reduced risk of obesity-related complications, such as heart disease and type II diabetes.
- Improved family dynamics and relationships.
- New friends and support group from the programme.

For parents:

- Raising healthier, happier children!
- Education about healthy eating and a foundation for a healthier lifestyle.
- Better understanding of the dangers and risks of obesity.
- An opportunity to take preventative action.

- Improved health.
- Understanding of behavioural management of children and creating a supportive environment.
- Improved family dynamics and relationships.
- New friends, and a support group of parents in the local area.

For more information on the MEND Programme visit:
www.mendprogramme.org

About the Author

Paul Sacher is a recognised expert in child health and obesity. He is a highly qualified and experienced Paediatric Nutrition Consultant who has improved the health and nutritional status of thousands of children through his publications and clinical work. He has worked as a specialist dietitian at Great Ormond Street Hospital for Children NHS Trust for five and a half years. He is now a Clinical Research Fellow at the Institute of Child Health where he is researching ways to improve the health of overweight and obese children. Paul is the founder of the MEND (mind, exercise, nutrition and diet) Programme, which is a lifestyle programme for overweight and obese children and their families. He is currently Chief Investigator of a large randomised controlled trial and his research has been peer-reviewed and published in scientific journals.

Paul has studied and worked on three different continents, where he has developed his unique, integrated clinical style. He has previously collaborated with two best-selling authors – Gina Ford on *The Contented Child's Food Bible* (Vermilion) and

Annabel Karmel on *Superfoods for Babies and Children* (Ebury Press). Paul acts as a consultant on nutritional matters to authors and child health-care experts in the publishing field as well as being a regular contributor to various publications. Paul regularly lectures to large groups of doctors, nurses, dietitians, other healthcare professionals and students.

Paul completed a BSc in medicine followed by a two-year postgraduate degree in Nutrition and Dietetics. He is currently undertaking a PhD in Child Health and works closely with world leaders in the field of paediatric nutrition. He is currently holder of a Department of Health, Researcher Development Award and his research work is also supported by the MRC Childhood Nutrition Research Centre at the Institute of Child Health and Great Ormond Street Hospital for Children. Paul is Public Relations Officer for the Paediatric Group of the British Dietetic Association and is registered with the Health Professions Council and is a member of the British Dietetic Association, the Association for the Study of Obesity and the Nutrition Society.

Testimonials

The following are some testimonials from participants in a previous MEND Programme:

'Very useful as we have learnt how to eat healthily as a family.' (Parent)

'MEND has taught me which foods I should eat more of and which foods are really bad for me.' (Nine-year-old child)

'I never thought I would see the day when (my child) would enjoy exercise.' (Parent)

'MEND has improved our family relationships so much.' (Parent)

For further information on the MEND Programme and to watch a short movie on the programme, please see: www.mendprogramme.org

Further Reading

The Contented Child's Food Bible,
Gina Ford and Paul Sacher (Vermilion, 2004).

Easy GI Diet, Helen Foster (Hamlyn, 2004).

Fit Kids, Mary L Gavin, Steven A Dowshen and Neil Izenberg (Dorling Kindersley, 2004).

The GI Diet, Rick Gallop (Virgin, 2002).

The Gi Plan, Azmina Govindji and Nina Puddefoot (Vermilion, 2004).

How to Help Your Overweight Child, Karen Sullivan (Rodale, 2004).

The Low GI Diet, Jennie Brand-Miller and Kaye Foster-Powell with Joanna McMillan-Price (Hodder, 2004).

Our Overweight Children, Sharron Dalton (University of California Press, 2004).

Useful Addresses & Resources

The MEND Programme

29 Cathedral Lodge, 110–115 Aldersgate Street, London EC1A 4JE.

Telephone: 0870 6091405 www.mendprogramme.org

The British Dietetic Association

5th Floor, Charles House, 148/9 Great Charles Street, Queensway,

Birmingham, B3 3HT.

www.bda.uk.com and www.weightwisebda.uk.com

British Nutrition Foundation

High Holborn House, 52-54 High Holborn, London,

WC1V 6RQ.

www.nutrition.org.uk

The Association for the Study of Obesity

20 Brook Meadow Close, Woodford Green, Essex, IG8 9NR.

www.aso.org.uk

The Food Standards Agency

England: Aviation House, 125 Kingsway, London, WC2B 6NH.

Scotland: St Magnus House, 6th Floor, 25 Guild Street, Aberdeen, AB11 6NJ.

Wales: 11th Floor, Southgate House, Wood Street, Cardiff, CF10 1EW

www.foodstandards.gov.uk and www.eatwell.gov.uk

The Obesity Awareness & Solutions Trust (TOAST)

The Latton Bush Centre, Southern Way, Harlow, Essex,
CM18 7BL. Telephone: 0845 0450225

www.toast-uk.org.uk

Great Ormond Street Hospital for Children and the Institute of Child Health

Great Ormond Street, London, WC1N 3JH.

www.gosh.nhs.uk

NHS Direct

Telephone: 0845 4647

www.nhsdirect.nhs.uk

Glycemic Index Research Service

www.glycemicindex.com

Carnegie Weight Management

www.carnegieweightmanagement.com

Weight Concern

Telephone: 020 7679 6636

www.weightconcern.com

Sustrans

Telephone: 0845 1130065

www.sustrans.org.uk

Index